This book drew me in and kept me turning the pages. 'Our Separated Lives' takes us beyond the facts of forced adoption and the societal norms of the day. It is written with heart wrenching honesty about the decisions that were made on Phil's behalf that left him totally stranded, humiliated, and confused.

As a birth mother from the forced adoption era, Phil's experiences touched me personally. I often say, "Adoption affects so many more people than just the mother and baby." Here we have a father's experience of the influence of family, friends and religion, and the government policies that tore young lives apart.

Written in an engaging open style with insights into adoption and social work practices past and present, 'Our Separated Lives' offers a vital new perspective on understanding the causes and consequences of adoption, and concludes with introspective open-ended questions about separated lives. A 'must read' for anyone touched by adoption.

Di Riddell
Author of 'Beyond Abuse' and
'Speak Out: From Suppression to Expression'

In exploring his journey, Phil has sought to better understand not only his own story as a father who lost a daughter to adoption in 1970, but also the experiences of adopted people. His motivation is clear: to build a stronger, more understanding relationship with his daughter, while walking alongside others in the adoption community. In doing so, he has quietly supported many adopted people and parents who have lost children to adoption—listening with empathy, sharing his perspective with humility, and asking thoughtful questions that reflect his genuine desire to learn.

Phil's book, 'Our Separated Lives', is an extension of the man himself—raw, honest, and unafraid to articulate the longing, complexity, and fragility of adoption and reunion. Many times while reading, I was moved to tears by the way he captures emotions that so many feel but cannot find the words to express. Phil's voice is one that matters in the adoption conversation, and I am grateful for his courage in sharing it.

Dr Jo-Ann Sparrow
President, Jigsaw Queensland

Congratulations Philip J Kenward on having the courage to share your story with the world. A powerful and compelling account, told with very real and raw emotion; I had to keep turning the page. I also enjoyed how Philip reminisced about his early childhood, especially the thunder box in the back yard and the lolly cigarettes.

I could relate to Philip's emotional journey, as I am married to one of those fathers whose first daughter was adopted at birth. Although his story is vastly different and one we don't often speak about, I recognise the same range of emotions in him.

I applaud, Phil, that the facts around forced adoption have been revealed, and can say from my own experience it was still practiced in 1975. I was also pressured coercively, but I was one of the lucky ones as my parents backed me to keep my son.
Thank you, Phil, for sharing such a powerful story.

Rita-Marie Lenton,
Funeral Celebrant and Author

"This powerful memoir highlights the pervasive impact of forced adoption, attachment, loss, shame, rejection, grief, parenthood, love and the stories that weave the webs of connection within us and between us."

Dr Cathrine Musaeus
Clinical Psychologist

OUR *Separated* LIVES

Philip J Kenward

Our Separated Lives
Copyright © 2025 Philip J Kenward
First published 2025

Disruptive Publishing
17 Spencer Avenue
Deception Bay QLD 4508
Australia
www.disruptivepublishing.com.au

Cover design by Sarah and Anna Kenward
Cover image by E.laine Photography
(@e.lainephotography) Instagram

All rights reserved. Without limiting the rights under Copyright reserved above, no part of this publication may be reproduced, stored in, or introduced into a database and retrieval system, or transmitted in any form or by any means (electronic, mechanical, photocopying, recording or otherwise) without the prior written permission of both the owner of the Copyright and the above publishers.

ISBN# 978-0-646-71531-5 Print
ISBN# 978-0-646-71752-4 eBook

DISCLAIMER

This book is a memoir, based on my memories, and on information and documents disclosed during the course of my research.

Our Separated Lives, articulates **my** experience of the events covered in this book.

No malice is intended to any person mentioned in this book.

Some names have been changed due to privacy or legal considerations.

OUR *Separated* LIVES

A FATHER'S STORY OF
FORCED ADOPTION

PHILIP J KENWARD

Comfortably Numb

When I was a child I caught a fleeting glimpse

Out of the corner of my eye

I turned to look but it was gone

I cannot put my finger on it now

The child is grown, the dream is gone

I have become **comfortably numb**

"Comfortably Numb" lyrics by Roger Waters
The Wall, Pink Floyd
1979 © Harvest/EMI (UK)
and Columbia/CBS Records (US)

Contents

Foreword 1

Preface 5

1 | Childhood 9

2 | Adolescence 21

3 | Beatle Boots And Paisley 31

4 | Intervention 41

5 | Losing It ... Big Time 51

6 | Staying Connected 59

7 | Birth Days 69

8 | The Visit to Boothville 77

9 | What Comes Next? 89

10 | A 'Clean Break' 97

11 | The Aftermath 109

12 | Travel Bugs 125

13 | Adoption Laws 137

14 | The Resurrection 147

15 | Meeting Up 157

16 | Meeting Up, Examined 169

17 | Where To From Here?	173
18 | It's Not An Easy Road	183
19 | Where Do I Fit In?	191
20 | Radio Silence	199
21 | Mental Incidentals	203
22 | Feelings	221
23 | Epilogue	235
Afterword	239
Resources	241
About the Author	243
Acknowledgements	245
What's next?	247
Get in Touch	247

Foreword

Forced adoption practices in Australia, particularly from the 1940s through to the 1980s, created a profound and lasting impact on the lives of hundreds of thousands of Australians. Babies were taken—often through coercion or misinformation—from their mothers and fathers and placed for adoption. The intent at the time was framed as being in "the best interests of the child," yet history has shown that these practices often severed vital family connections, erased identities, and caused enduring grief and trauma.

In 2012 and 2013, national and Queensland apologies acknowledged this injustice. For some, these apologies were a milestone in recognition and validation; for others, they were a bittersweet reminder of loss without tangible redress. In every case, they highlighted that the impacts of adoption do not fade—they are lived, every day, across generations.

Within the adoption community, certain voices have historically been heard more often than others. Mothers who lost children to adoption have led much of the public advocacy and storytelling, while the experiences of adopted people have become increasingly visible in recent years. But there is another perspective that is still too rarely heard—the perspective of fathers.

Some fathers were denied a say in the fate of their children. Others, caught in the norms and pressures of their time, avoided or deflected their responsibilities. Some used their influence to compel an adoption, while others yearned for a place in their child's life but were shut out entirely. Each of these stories is shaped by the social attitudes, personal circumstances, and human frailty of the time. They are stories of complexity—sometimes of regret, sometimes of reconciliation, always of humanity.

This book by Phil Kenward offers such a perspective. It is a father's voice—honest, searching, and layered with the emotional nuance that comes from living with an adoption story over decades. Phil's writing reflects the challenges of reunion: the constant mental balancing of one's own needs with those of the other person; the careful negotiation of relationship boundaries; the frustration of mismatched paces when one heart wants more and the other is cautious; and the reality that some divides, however earnestly bridged, may never be fully closed.

As an adopted person, peer support worker and as President of Jigsaw Queensland, I have witnessed how sharing these personal stories creates space for understanding, healing, and connection. A father's voice like Phil's expands our collective picture of adoption's impact. It reminds us that reconciliation is not an event but an ongoing process—a commitment to empathy, patience, and hope.

May this work encourage more fathers to speak, more families to listen, and more of us to approach the ongoing story of adoption with the compassion and openness it deserves.

Dr Jo-Ann Sparrow
President, Jigsaw Queensland

Preface

How does one deal with loss? What is loss, and how does it define you? Loss, as you will see, can take many forms.

For me, the 10th of November 1970 was a pivotal day. I was sixteen years old, and my girlfriend Fran—who was eighteen years of age—had just given birth to our daughter. Not that I knew this, of course, as I was being kept in the dark ... I didn't even know where she was.

My life would never be the same again, and this day would have a very long-lasting effect on me.

Writing this book at the age of seventy-one has given me time to reflect—with clear memories—on what has come, and what has gone; on how you can lose control over the things that are most precious to you. What it's like to be a spectator watching as your life gets ruined by people who think they are doing the right thing by you ... and you are powerless to do anything about it! Fuck those people, fuck them all for the long-term damage and mental anguish they inflicted on me when I was *so* young! *Their* actions changed *my* life forever.

Am I hanging onto loss and grief? Oh, God yes! And it won't let me go. This is not something that can be brushed aside easily. Loss and grief continue to have a good and proper grip on me, but I've made my peace, and I know I can't change the past; it is what it is.

I'm writing this from the perspective of the father who lost a child from her birth date, when she was adopted against my (our) will.

I've never read a word about how this type of thing might affect a father. There are lots of stories, books published, and even dedicated television programs, and podcasts about adoption throughout the world depicting lovely reunions between mothers and their sons and daughters. It all looks so wonderful, but I can tell you … it is not always like this.

In the case of adoption, very rarely does the father get mentioned. So, I am also telling my story on behalf of the fathers of the 9798 children who were adopted in 1970 in Australia. Every one of those children had a father … Where are they now? Where is their voice? What is their story? These individuals must be around my vintage too, if not a little younger or a little older. Who speaks for them? Are they *all* hiding? It's very, very quiet …

Some fathers may have had contact and reunion experiences, but many would not. Some of these reunions may have gone well with an excellent outcome, but many would not. If you look at the adoption figures in Australia from 1971 to 1972 you find they were the highest on record (the height of the Forced Adoption period). There was an increase in adoptions that year of

Preface

forty-five percent over the previous four years. Since then, adoption numbers have decreased; for example, in the period 1975-1976 there were 4990. In 1979-1980 the number was 3337. In 1995 it sat at a total of 668. The latest figures from 2020-2021 indicate 264 adoptions, which shows a sixty-three percent decline from 1996-1997. The trend is ever downward which marks a huge change in the way society itself looks at adoptions in this country. (Source: www.aihw.gov.au)

So, considering all of that I'm now going to tell you my story.

1 | Childhood

I'd say my childhood was pretty standard for an Aussie kid. Eat, sleep, rinse, repeat.

School, pushbikes, swimming, slot cars, becoming a father ... what else would you expect at the tender age of 16? Life had just begun ...

And church on Sundays—there was always church on Sundays. Boring! As a kid I used to get picked up for Sunday school by the always jovial Mr Rafferty. He drove a vintage 1950's Morris Z Ute and would turn up with his black pinstriped waistcoat over his checked shirt, a dickie bow tie, and a flat cap on. An equally smiling Mrs Rafferty would usually occupy the passenger seat; she was a rather rotund woman, smartly attired in a floral-patterned dress with her straw hat on top. She also had stockings on her legs rolled down to the knee but in full view below the hemline of her dress—like long socks, but not. An odd sight to see.

We kids, probably up to six of us, picked up from various surrounding suburbs, would perch ourselves either side in the back of the small ute. We sat on wooden planks, with a short handrail behind us, for the trip to church—no seatbelts in those days. I saw all of my time at church as marking time, clock-watching until I could get out of there. I was never attentive to being preached at, and to me there were far more important things to be occupying my time.

The Fourth Avenue house; off to Sunday school in the Morris Z ute

I spent an inordinate amount of time at the swimming pool at Sandgate, a suburb north of Brisbane, Queensland. This was a saltwater pool complex built between Fourth and Fifth Avenues, probably 500 to 600 metres south from where the current pool complex is situated. Built in 1929, it was also notable for its high concrete façade painted in a whitewashed finish and highlighted with tall, dark blue parapets at each corner. The pool, and surrounding above-ground structure, jutted out into the ocean and it was quite a feat of engineering.

It was owned and run by a family who lived next door to us in Fourth Avenue. Anyone who lived in Sandgate and went to the pool knew Harry the proprietor—he was a grumpy old bugger. There was an air of snobbery about

1 | CHILDHOOD

that family; they thought they were a class above us and rarely engaged in conversation with us *commoners*. The price of admission to the pool was 1 bob (10 cents).

The pool itself was filled by the sea through huge sluice gates at the rear of the complex as high tide washed in, and was occasionally drained at low tide for maintenance. The pool's capacity was 205,500 gallons (934,000 litres) of water. Huge bags of lime for water treatment were stored onsite to douse the sea water. The water was never actually clear; it always had a sort of murkiness and thickness to it.

There was a sloping timber sun-bathing deck which ran the full length of the pool and overlooked it. Access stairs to the deck were at each end, and there were also single change rooms below the deck. The whitewashed theme was carried throughout, with multicoloured doors on the change rooms and service areas.

I'd spend hours up there on the deck in the harshest of sunshine, talking to my mates and lying face down on my towel, burning my back to a crisp. Sheets of skin would peel off my back and shoulders in the following weeks. It was a bit like a badge I wore that cast me as a surfie/coastal-type dude. In all the years I was there I never, ever put sun tan cream on, not once—that was for pussies! My hair was always stiff, unruly, and bleached blonde, partly from the sun and probably from the chemical mixture doused in the pool water. I was scared to death of talking to girls, although there would have been one or two that sparked my attention, usually blonde, usually in a fluoro-coloured bikini!

Swimming carnivals were held year-round at the pool, even when the lice were biting at their very worst. I was a member of the local swimming club. Even on freezing cold winter nights, with an offshore wind cutting through and giving us goosebumps the size of pimples, we'd take our place on the starting blocks and dive into the icy water to compete in our events.

One night we lined up on the angled starting blocks in my first handicap freestyle event, my favourite stroke. An official walked behind each of us giving us our handicap number—the only trouble is I didn't actually know what that meant!! Not long after, a starting gun fired and the numbers started to be called, so I left my starting block and ran around to ask Mum on the sidelines what seven meant. She quickly informed me that I was to go on the call of seven. I then raced back to my block just in time to make my number, dived in and swam like a boy possessed, trying against all odds to catch the leaders. Impossible odds, I was a good swimmer, but not that good.

The low tide at Sandgate left behind in its wake the mud flats, which meant you could walk out about five-hundred metres towards the retreating sea on the exposed sand, for the length of Flinders Parade— probably five kilometres or more. The tide going out every twelve hours saw soldier crabs by the thousands

1 | CHILDHOOD

roaming the sand out in the open. As kids we used to run amongst their packs, spreading them far and wide. If you got too close the little creatures would burrow quickly beneath the surface and disappear instantaneously. It was like a game of hide and seek—wait long enough and the crabs would reappear, only to be chased once again.

Fishermen loved low tide as well as it gave them an opportunity to pump for yabbies. Yabby pumps were hand-held devices plunged into the sand, which would suck up a cylinder of the wet soil. They would then pump it out onto the surface to find the small crustaceans they would use for bait.

Along the waterfront there were vast puddles, which weren't very deep, left by the outgoing tide. As kids we used to skim board along these rivulets. Skim boarding was popular in the late '60s, and used a circular board made of marine-grade plywood about 600mm in diameter, which was lacquered to a high polish. You'd run along at speed through the shallows, skim board between your hands, then throw the board in front and leap on it to ride it surfboard style. The rides were short but exhilarating! Sometimes you might step on a stingray on your run up. They'd be trapped in the shallows, slightly buried, and it would come as a hell of a shock as they were so well camouflaged. Fortunately, they were quick to scurry away with their wings flapping madly and long tail giving them direction.

There were also four or five single changing sheds on the

waterfront reserved for the Catholic nuns to use. The sheds were timber slatted on the exterior with a small, corrugated-iron pitched roof, and padlocked doors front and rear. They sat on stumps with a ramp for entry off a stone wall, then a set of stairs at the rear to exit into the sea. Privacy for the nuns was of utmost importance!

My uncle and aunty owned a kiosk nearby where they served Devonshire teas and other treats. Uncle Tim was an expert at making toffee apples—he lined them up on a marble slate top for the bright, red-hot toffee to cool and glaze, such a sugary delight which sold for a few pence each.

Across the road from the pool, and under the imposing structure of the Empire Flats, was another takeaway café. It had a counter with large jars, chock-full of lollies of every kind, on display. For ten cents you could fill your small paper bag with quite a variety. Columbines, Fantales, Milk Bottles, Wizz Fizz's, Sherbert Cones, and Choo-choo bars to name but a few. There were even Fags, confectionery which looked like a lit smoke, ha ha!

As for school, I basically had no interest. It just took up time between play. My early school years don't hold many notable memories for me; however, one incident did scar me. I used to happily bring schoolmates home, and we'd sit on the back stairs, hoeing into huge slices of watermelon … until my mother appeared at the top of the stairs one day and asked all of my mates if they'd been circumcised like I had. I was mortified and turned as red as the watermelon. How embarrassing.

1 | CHILDHOOD

Me, in The Boys' Brigade Uniform

Further along Flinders Parade from our place stood a massive house, dowdy and uninviting in appearance. This was officially the Sandgate Maternal and Child Welfare Home—but locally we referred to it as the Sandgate Childrens' Home—run by the Department of Health, as the sign facing the road stated. The imposing structure filled the expansive block of land. It had two sets of wide stairs leading up to different sections of the building and high, corrugated style roofing above, but its most notable feature were rows of casement timber windows facing the road. It also had tall, Besser Block walls along its forward-facing boundary, secluding the inhabitants from the outside world.

The staff here wore nursing uniforms: white shirts and blue tunics. The children attended school in Sandgate and had to choose from folded piles of second-hand clothing to wear each day. The home was a refuge for children whose mothers had suffered serious illness, including mental trauma. The home was also utilised to help 'bush children', some of whom may have been *stolen generation*—displaced aboriginal kids—forcibly removed from their family and institutionalised here. I can neither confirm or validate this, but it points to the shameful government meddling of the time. Where children were found to have been abandoned, Children's Services would make them wards of the state.

The children were taken out for afternoon walks along the waterfront, but this was no ordinary walk—it was military-style. Kids of all ages lined up in rows and frog-marched, with the staff at the front and back herding them. Some of the smaller children were tethered to an adult with a shoulder harness and lead. It always seemed to be an interesting site, with lots of goings-on and it was definitely different from the 'normal' outside world. There are many stories online of the hard and cruel treatment dished out by the nurses or sisters too.

I attended ballroom dancing classes at the Sandgate town hall one afternoon a week. The dance teacher was 6' 5" (195 cm) tall and towered over us. He wore notably loose-fitting flared trousers (lots of room for movement in there), tight silk shirts with a silk paisley cravat around his neck, and his shoes were at least as pointy as his nose was. He made dancing look easy as he floated through the air with his ever-so-charming steps and stiff upper frame.

We'd pair up with girls to dance with and I'd always flush red in the face throughout the whole performance. Often the teacher would grab me and lead the way he wanted the dance to go—he'd play the part of the girl, and the penance for a mistake was him stomping on your feet

1 | CHILDHOOD

with those oversized pointy shoes. I went on to dance in competitions and won individual medallions with my dance partner, Dianne. We'd also appear as a dance troupe of eight on television in Jim Iliffe's *The Channel Niners* afternoon show several times a year. For our TV appearances I was dressed in long grey dress shorts to my knees, long socks (which also met my shorts at my knees) above highly polished shoes, a white dress shirt with a bow tie that was strangling me, and an overly wide, pink cummerbund around my waist. Mum made sure my hair was tacked down by spitting on her hand, pressing my curly fringe into place before I left home.

The girls wore flared dresses—so much easier to wear, I'm sure. It was the era of black and white TV, so at least no one knew my cummerbund was pink. As far as I know our dance performances were near perfect and no mistakes were made, a testament to practicing them week-in-and-week-out. I can recall how very cold it was on the actual set. Maybe the air conditioning was set so low (it was freezing) so we didn't sweat. Who knows? We'd all come off the set with a huge sense of relief, but also of a job well done, phheeeww! Our dance team seemed to work very well, and I don't recall why I left, as I did enjoy it.

Speaking of TV's, one of my young friend's parents had acquired a television in 1961; a bit of a rarity back then. My family didn't get a TV until many years later. A 21-inch TV set would cost around $490 (an equivalent of $4,700 today) and there were only three channels available:

QTQ 9, BTQ 7, and ABC 2. The television set—a small screen by today's standards of flat screens—was considered a piece of furniture to enhance the lounge room.

I used to get invited one night a week to go to my friend's flat and watch some cartoons. I'd be all bathed and tidy in my pyjamas, dressing gown, and slippers, and I'd make my way to his flat which was on the third floor of the old, tenanted block between Third and Fourth Avenues. The Empire Café flats were home to lots of 'poor' working-class people; the corridors reeked of smoke and the walls were either discoloured or in need of repair on every level of the old building. Lots of strange noises emanated from behind those doors. I found it quite scary making my way in and out of the building as the hallways were either dimly lit or had no light at all, and the floorboards creaked.

Where are our slippers?

As a kid of about eight or nine years I didn't see a lot of my dad as he was always working shiftwork. One Saturday morning I felt privileged that he asked me to tag along with him. We walked the short distance to the Sandgate railway station, with Dad toting a heavy, hessian sack full of brass and copper offcuts he'd collected over a period. The journey into Albion was in

1 | CHILDHOOD

'the rattlers'—very old, maroon-painted train carriages built of timber—which lurched and moved around a lot due to their age. The carriages had a series of big outward swinging doors with glass windows in the centre and huge, polished brass handles on the outside for passenger entry and exit. Inside were rows of red vinyl bench seats facing each other. You usually had to wipe the seats off with a handkerchief, before sitting, to remove the coal dust so your clothes didn't get filthy. A white handkerchief wouldn't be white for long.

These carriages were pulled by an old-style coal-fired steam locomotive, but diesel engines weren't too far away into the future. They could still get up a head of speed though, and the movement of the old carriages creaked and groaned as we travelled. If you let the window down and hung your head out in the open air you would cop an eyeful or a mouthful of coal soot.

Once Dad's cache of metal was separated, then weighed, and money changed hands at the metal recycling merchant, we'd walk back up the hill to one of the pubs in Albion. Dad would leave me perched outside while he went in, presumably for a beer, although he was never really a drinker. Maybe he saw this as part of his reward, or maybe he just wanted a little more time for himself away from the responsibility of the other four kids at home. If he was there long enough, I'd be given a large icy lemonade while Dad went back inside. The trip home on the train would be mostly the same as the trip in: sitting in silence, as Dad didn't ever have too much to say, to me at least.

It may seem a bit strange, but I think I had a strong sense of right and wrong from a very early age, highlighted by an incident at our house on Flinders Parade. The exterior weatherboard finish was looking a bit dated, so Dad decided to get some quotes to fix it. Two men appeared at the back door one afternoon claiming the product they were touting, 'Benelux', was the ultimate in exterior finishes. They were invited in to show my parents some glossy brochures.

Now, this pair were dressed in business shirts with ties, and trousers which had seen better days. Their shoes looked like they'd trudged the suburbs forever, and they had slicked-back Brylcreem hair—very shady indeed. They were doing the hard sell on Mum and Dad and got a cash deposit out of them right away for several hundred dollars. Even from the next room I quicky sensed that this pair were charlatans in every way, but I couldn't understand why my parents, wise of worldly things I thought, were not picking up on this couple of rats. Mum and Dad ended up paying thousands of dollars for very little end gain and were right royally ripped off.

2 | Adolescence

Between fourteen and fifteen years-of-age lots of things were happening. I was an enthusiastic teenager with energy to burn. Dad asked me to help him thin out a patch of banana trees in the backyard one day. Dad would cut down the thick trunks of the banana trees, I'd then stand across them, in my thongs, wielding an axe and flailing it about all over the place. I wasn't taking any of this really seriously and found this out when the axe went wayward and I hit myself in the shin with a glancing blow. No blood, bruised perhaps, so I carried on with great enthusiasm.

The next errant blow nearly lopped off the little toes on my right foot. I screamed blue murder and hobbled as quickly as possible into the house with blood from my foot spurting all over the place. Mum just washed my wound under a tap, then wrapped it up in a makeshift bandage. We never went to the doctor! A filthy axe-head covered in plant and soil matter, a gaping wound right down to the bone ... what could possibly go wrong? The throbbing soon subsided, and it looked like I'd survive and not get sepsis or require an amputation. 'Twas just a flesh wound, thank God for that!

The banana patch was right next to the outdoor loo (aptly

named the thunderbox) in the days when a trip to the toilet meant walking right up the backyard, doing the doings, then covering it with fresh sawdust (the wood shavings smelled really good) from a pile next to the loo. Sometimes if we didn't have toilet paper Mum would cut old newspapers into squares and hang them from a piece of string—newspaper isn't soft I can tell you. There was no flushing the contents away; the buckets were picked up by a truck in the early morning once a week by a crew going house-to-house. They ran, carrying the buckets on their shoulders to deposit them into the truck. Fortunately for them they carried a stock of lids to place over the top of the buckets.

Another time I was under the high-set house we lived in at Fourth Avenue and fiddled with a couple of open wires that were hanging down. I wondered what would happen if I held an end in each hand. I found out very quickly after feeling the surge of 240 volts of electricity coursing through my upper body before I was thrown at least ten feet away to the ground, probably with my hair still smoking at one end and my toes tingling at the other. What a shock! I didn't tell anyone about this either, I just got up brushed myself off and carried on. Maybe that's what's wrong with me: too many volts!!

There was a randy teenage girl who lived with her middle-income parents three doors down from us, and they thought they were a cut above the rest of us. I used to play with her little brother, even though he annoyed the shit out of me. He had every toy and every game known

2 | ADOLESCENCE

to the living universe, the latest dragster pushbike, etc., but he was an aggravating little twat.

One day, at their place, his sister had a definite strategy to get me alone. She made short work of getting rid of her brother and whispered to me that she wanted to play 'mothers and fathers' with me. I actually had no idea what she was on about but followed her as she led me by the hand to underneath a table in a room under the house. It had a long tablecloth draped over its sides providing a modicum of cover. Seated cross-legged facing each other in the semi-dark she was quick to lift up her dress with one hand and pull her knickers down with the other. My temperature was rising as she said you can touch 'it' if you like! My biggest, and only, concern was getting caught like this red-handed—as it were—so I did what any uneasy teenage boy would do and hit the tow and ran home.

I used to chat to one of my neighbours in the communal laundry of her block of flats next door on a regular basis. Why? I have no idea, but I was probably trying to make sense of the world. So, a few days later I told her what had happened; I think I was still trying to make sense of the under-the-table episode. Why would I want to touch that thing? The mid-forties female neighbour laughed uproariously, and I was still none the wiser.

The Sandgate picture theatre, or the 'Beach Theatre' as it was known, was only one block away from our house and a source of much enjoyment. The old building had been there since 1924 and had had several upgrades over the years. The front of the building facing Flinders Parade was half the block wide, and looked nearly as tall, with a huge, suspended awning covering the footpath, outlined by a row of fancy light bulbs. On the fascia, giant-sized billboards displayed animated pictures of the feature films currently showing. Inside the bi-fold glass doors the ticket booth was to the left: a timber structure with a small counter that had a glass window with a hole cut in it, where a worker passed customers their tickets.

The Sandgate Beach Theatre
(Courtesy Sandgate & District Historical Society)

A large popcorn making machine sat behind a central counter and a sweets kiosk was to the right. You could buy packets of chips, ice creams, and lollies like White Knights, Polly Waffles, Redskins and Gobstoppers. There was a popular lounge area which was packed with people young and old. The price of admission was two shillings or twenty cents.

Dad took me to see all of the James Bond films starring

2 | Adolescence

Sean Connery (the only real 007). We sat upstairs in the 'dress circle', with the luxury of carpet on the floor and plush seats, etc. The seats below in 'general admission' were a laid-back affair comprising of a timber frame with hessian sacking material forming the very relaxing seating position.

At the times I did frequent the downstairs stalls I was usually with my mates. I was once smacked in the side of the head by some big bruiser behind me just because I was there and for no other reason. Another time I had a cigarette lighter lit under my bum, probably by the same bully. It was enough to have me squirming at first, then as the heat intensified, I had to stand and yell, *Aarrgghh!!* This would usually have the cinema's attendant come running down the aisle, torch in hand, to throw me out for making too much noise. They weren't interested in hearing my side of the story; I was gone, out for being a troublemaker. People used to roll marbles or Jaffas down the sloping timber floor for fun too. A waste of a good Jaffa if you ask me.

Another time at the movies I met up with a girl from school. She had a lovely boho-style flared skirt, which proved to be perfect to spread out and hide our handholding under its broad pleats. She was leading the charge, not sweet innocent me. It was probably just as well that it was dark in there, as it hid my face blushing the brightest red. It also hid our hands from the attendant who'd walk the aisles checking with her torch that there was no mischief occurring on her watch. There definitely was no tomfoolery going on as far as I was concerned. Needless to say, I wasn't asked for a second date. She probably wanted to smooch, very forward of her, but I was far more interested in the action on the screen, which had really gotten me in. Such a big screen.

Unfortunately, in 1978 the old picture theatre burned down and could not be saved. It was later demolished to make way for unit accommodation. Maybe it was that bugger trying to set my bum alight.

Speaking of smooching … my young cousins from Sydney, Timothy, Beryl, and Christoper, used to visit my uncle and aunty in Sandgate every Christmas. Timothy was the wise, older brother, a very sensible chap. Christoper was the absolute opposite and was always into mischief; a real-life rascal, forever in trouble, and he would try and lead me astray as well. Beryl, on the other hand, was a looker and such a girly girl. One day we were playing across at the beachfront from my parents' house—God knows what we were playing at. Beryl then called me in behind a huge Moreton Bay fig tree out of view. I wondered what she could have wanted, but it soon became apparent when she said, "Do you want to kiss?"

I was really gun-shy of girls, but thought why not? Man, that turned into the *sweeeetest* kiss I'd ever had! It was, after all, my first and only kiss at the time. It must have left its mark because I can still remember it to this day fifty-seven years later. *Sidenote*: my cousin Beryl and I

2 | ADOLESCENCE

didn't see each other from that point until we reconnected fifty years later.

On the opposite corner to the picture theatre was a biker's café: greasy hamburgers and milkshakes all round—no alcohol on these sort of premises in those days. Late on Friday and Saturday nights hundreds of bikers would descend and park their bikes along the length of Flinders Parade and around the corner into Fourth Avenue. I was totally intrigued by this carry-on as I watched from the safety of my bedroom window a little up the road—curtain twitching. Bodgies and Widgies in black leather and denim were really strutting it, black and chrome bikes of every make, mostly American Harleys or British iron. Most were parked up against the kerb, some were just left wherever they liked, even in the middle of the road, regardless of the consequences. Lots were lined up, drag racing or roaring at high speed along the waterfront with their hair flowing freely in the breeze, as there were no helmet laws then. The bikers smoked like chimneys, with fags hanging off their lips as the girls cooed over them. I loved it, the image, every last bit of it especially the rebelliousness of it all, the smell of burnt rubber and hot engines.

One of our neighbours also rode a bike, an old Matchless 500. He used to visit his girlfriend a couple of nights a week in the old flats next door. He then replaced the Matchy with a brand-spanking new Triumph Bonneville 650, although this didn't last long when he found out his girlfriend was pregnant. I wonder what caused that??

Remembering my innocence. While he had the new bike I used to greet him in the afternoons for a chat about it. I think I was hoping some of his 'coolness' might rub off onto me.

He was a really nice guy, had the image, the slicked-back hair, the black beard, leather Brando-style jacket, and well-used denim jeans. And it was certainly the right bike finished in silver and maroon paint on the tank with gold pinstriping and acres of chrome accessories. Pity that didn't last as he settled down to family life and raising a child. A lesson in life right there.

Little did I know then that motorcycles would play such a huge part in my life to come.

Another high school friend, Peter, and I used to go regularly to the Brisbane Exhibition Speedway on a Saturday night. We'd catch the train into Fortitude Valley, then on the way out of the station, Peter would bravely buy a single panatela cigar from a tobacconist nearby. No questions were asked about if he was old enough; then we'd light it up and smoke our way through this gigantic fat stick of smoke. It was more likely I coughed my way through it, but I was trying to look as cool as shit.

Next stop, the Chinese restaurant just up the road. It had a row of cooked and glazed dead ducks hanging freely outside its façade, swaying in the breeze of the passing traffic on Brunswick Street. The delight of sweet and sour pork—in a takeaway container with two plastic forks—tasted so exotic compared to our usual home

2 | ADOLESCENCE

cooked staple of meat and three vegies boiled to death in a pressure cooker every God-damned night. The Chinese food was probably full of msg, but we couldn't have cared less. We ate as we walked, sharing the pleasure of the delicious sauces.

The smell of methanol racing fuel filled the air soon enough. A night of solo motorcycles, sidecars, midget and compact speed cars. The finale was usually the V8 powered monster Sprint cars with their giant wings, spitting blue flames from their huge exhaust. The wind that hit your body, and the clumps of dirt, as the cars passed on each lap was incredible. It was pretty wild, and I loved it all. Racing cars were also soon to figure for me, but this would become a short-lived fantasy.

Little did innocent, happy-go-lucky, naïve me know it, but there was a storm coming, and at sixteen years old I wasn't prepared—through lack of life experience—for what was going to come next. I didn't have the mental capacity to deal with the responsibilities which were soon to be thrust upon me. I would have to grow up very, very quickly, which would deprive me of my real teenage years, and shape my future self for years to come.

While all this was happening, the world continued at pace. 1970 would see The Beatles split up after releasing their number one hit, 'Let It Be'. The Apollo 13 space mission was notable for the message the crew sent back to earth exclaiming, "Houston, we've had a problem," when one of their oxygen tanks exploded. Jimi Hendrix was found dead in a London apartment. It was all happening.

3 | BEATLE BOOTS AND PAISLEY

I was a pretty normal teenager, hung around with my mates in the seaside town of Sandgate north of Brisbane, rode push bikes everywhere, spent lots of time slot car racing and drove noisy old cars like Morris Minors, FB Holdens, and Hillman Minx's. During my early years I was involved in the Baptist Church at Sandgate, which included being a member of The Boys' Brigade church-based program. I might have even been considered a *goody two-shoes*; I certainly was not a trouble maker by any stretch of the imagination.

My parents were immigrants, or 'Ten Pound Poms', from Hastings on the south coast of England. Hastings is famous for the Battle of Hastings in 1066 where King Harold II copped an arrow to the eye which ultimately killed him. It may be a little-known fact, but the Battle of Hastings wasn't fought in Hastings itself, but in the small, historic town of Battle about ten kilometres from the seaside haven of Hastings. The town of Hastings is actually more renowned for being a smugglers' cove and still has remnants along its stony beachfront of these very activities.

Mum and Dad had lived through World War II. Being an ambulance driver, Dad was sent to Palestine—something he never talked about ... ever. Mum, who was ensconced at home in Bexhill on England's south coast, heard many hundreds of German aircraft loaded with their clutch of deadly ammunition fly overhead heading for bombing raids over the capital, London. Hiding in a cupboard underneath the staircase with her family, my fifteen-year-old mother would listen intently to the sound of the deadly V1 bombs flying directly above her.

My Dad, my hero (left)

They were nicknamed the Doodlebugs or Buzz bombs because of the distinctive sound of their Pulsejet engine. These bombs, sent from Germany, had random and unspecific targets and approximately eight-thousand of them were deployed between 1944 and 1945 (2419 hit London). They always worried when the sound of the bomb's rocket engine stopped due to running out of fuel—it could land nearby. Her father, my grandfather, was killed by one such errant bomb while he was on duty with the local fire brigade.

I was five years old when we emigrated by ship on the P&O line *T.S.S. Strathaird*, which sailed from Southampton in England to Sydney in 1958. The Strathaird had some history as it had been used as a

3 | Beatle Boots and Paisley

troopship during World War II and was then converted back to a passenger liner afterwards.

At this time our family consisted of Mum and Dad, my younger sister and me. On arrival we caught a train from Sydney to Brisbane to be reunited with my Uncle Tim and Aunty Ann. They had emigrated some years earlier and encouraged my parents to come out to Queensland to find a better life. They owned and ran a kiosk at Sandgate along the waterfront. The following years would see my dad working hard as a fitter machinist in various locations, while Mum looked after our newly-expanded family of five kids, of which I was the eldest.

Emigrating in 1957

When I first met Fran she was seventeen years old. I was sixteen years old and was finishing year ten at Sandgate District State High School. I hated school and couldn't wait to leave; my grades in all subjects were not good. I actually believed that I was stupid, but I know now, as my career would prove, that I am a long, long way from stupid. My problem was that I'd get left behind and no teacher ever really picked up on this so, naturally, I floundered.

I grew up in a time when corporal punishment was the norm in schools. Even back then I would have considered myself a lover and not a fighter, but sometimes I just had to defend myself. I got involved in several scuffles at school—which were usually not my fault—but then got caught by a passing teacher which would then see me hauled up to the principal's office.

Mr Arthur Vice was a cruel and nasty man who loved dispensing justice to students. He would summarily make you wait outside his office for an absolute age while he faffed about with paperwork and phone calls, only serving to heighten the tension of the punishment to come. Once called into the office you were stood to attention in front of his large timber desk. It was a thing of beauty, the centrepiece of the room, polished dark wood with lighter carvings around the edges, a dark green leather embossed top trimmed with gold leaf, everything on it precisely placed.

Mr Vice would pass comment that you knew what you had done wrong and why you were there—guilty. No number of excuses on my part would lessen his ire towards me. I knew what was coming, and he knew what was coming, but he played it up just a bit longer to extend the pain.

He did this by trying out several of his assorted canes that he'd retrieve from a circular stand next to his desk. He'd sort through, pick out a cane, bend it almost in half to test its flexibility, take a couple of swipes through the air and then return it to the holder. Next cane, then the next until he was happy with his choice. Then came

3 | Beatle Boots and Paisley

justice, but he gave you a choice: six to one hand or three on each. I usually chose six to my left hand to get it over with. Mr Vice's precision in dispensing 'the cuts' was never very accurate, sometimes he'd catch the tips of your fingers. Either way your hand was left marked, bruised black and blue, and swollen. It was difficult to get the movement back into your fingers, but move them you must. I can still recall the pain. My parents would never know about the punishment I received.

The winds of change to a new era of non-violence at Sandgate High must have started, as corporal punishment stopped by the time I had reached year nine or ten. Instead of the cuts, or cane, your penalty was to be 'kept in'. This meant spending even MORE time at the dreaded school—usually writing lines after-hours. They say where there's a will there's a way. As dumb as I thought I was, I came up with the idea of sticky taping four or five pens together, which in turn wrote you out four to five lines of text all at once. Bingo!! I think the teachers were onto this, but they couldn't care less as we were probably wasting their time too.

I disliked school work so much I decided to join the Army Cadets, which had a regiment within the school. This little side hustle would see me get out of more classes and provide some fun to boot. We did all the usual things like marching practice and drills, and were taught how to look after our uniform and kit, etc., so it was pretty disciplined. We also did target practice using .22 calibre live rounds on a rifle range at the school—can you imagine that these days?!

The Army Cadets also had a marching band, so I volunteered for that too. I took up drumming, which wasn't as easy as it looked when you had to keep step *and* hold a beat. The snare drum was placed onto your left thigh on a wide strap over your right shoulder, it all had to be adjusted to be comfortable whilst marching. I loved this newfound outlet of music. During my two years in the cadets, we also went on army camps to give us a real taste of army life. Like being dragged out of your tent at 2 a.m. in the pouring rain to do a full-pack ten-kilometre route march—great, sloshing about in the mud!

I also used to do a milk run on Friday nights with Mr Montgomery, an Irish milkman who lived up the road from us. I never actually knew his first name. We'd leave at around 10 p.m. and drive to a depot in Windsor to load up his canopied ute. We'd put so many crates of glass-bottled milk in the back and on top that the tail of the car would be dragging on the road. I'd travel sitting on the tailgate, with my feet up and hanging on for dear life as we whizzed around the streets. The ute would stop abruptly, Mr Montgomery would jump out of the driver's seat, grab a wire rack, which I would have loaded with six full bottles, and take off on foot into the dark.

I'd do likewise to the houses on the opposite side, sometimes battling errant dogs or running into huge spider webs. We used to go all night long, barely a word being said, delivering milk and collecting the cash left

3 | Beatle Boots and Paisley

out for us, then we'd return to the depot to unload the empties and reload the ute for the next trip. We'd do these runs three to four times until the early hours, watching the dawn rise as we finished. All this lifting and carrying and running made me as strong as an ox. I'd get home at around 6 a.m. happy with the ten dollars I'd made, have a couple of hours of restless sleep and start my day.

During Christmas holidays I worked night shift alongside my dad for a few weeks, and a few bucks, at a valve manufacturing facility in Geebung. Night shift was good, there were fewer people around, probably half the usual daytime staff, and no supervisors or bosses. It was pretty easy—if not monotonous—work producing machined valve bodies and other components by the hundred on lathes big and small over the length of an eight-hour shift. It was a funny environment to work in as well, as a league of nations worked there. Halfway through the night a call would go out in a thick Scottish accent, "It won't be long now …," and another call from the other end of the factory, in broad Yugoslav, would repeat it.

Dad also used to let me drive his 1958 Chevrolet Biscayne home in the early hours of the morning since the traffic was pretty light, even though I had no learner's permit or licence. This was quite the treat. She was a beautiful big American car, with two-tone green and cream paint, acres of bodywork, big, valanced guards and leather interior. That 4.6 litre, 235 cubic inch 'Blue flame' motor just purred along. The gearbox was three-on-the-tree, or column shift, and the clutch was very heavy and long-travel. It looked great and had a lot of street cred. I thought I was so cool driving that car. Unfortunately, it went under in the 1974 Brisbane floods and was no more.

I was still attending The Boys' Brigade on a Friday night with my mates and had achieved the rank of Lance Corporal. I was now in charge of a squad of younger boys and had an arm patch full of many badges I'd earnt through The Boys' Brigade attainment scheme.

I wasn't really into religion, or church for that matter. The thing that did attract me was the two Anderson sisters who started attending church on Sunday mornings, their slender legs sheathed in tight miniskirts. It seemed like a good enough excuse to attend. That and listening to the older boys talk after church about how they'd had sex; they probably hadn't, it was all talk and blowing hot air.

Up until now none of the other girls at church dared to wear anything as risqué as these two had. Tartan miniskirts, figure hugging blouses, silk stockings, high heeled shoes, long, flowing hair. They wore the height of fashion as opposed to the long knee-length dresses and flat sandals the other girls wore, with their hair up in a bun. Very dowdy!

Seeing the Anderson girls made me up the ante in the dress stakes too. My Grandmother, who lived in the UK, had recently sent out presents for all of us and within

3 | Beatle Boots and Paisley

Pink paisley and Beatle boots

that package was a pink paisley-patterned shirt with matching tie for me. Paisley was apparently all the rage in the fashion hub of Europe at the time. I'm not sure it ever took on here though as men's formal wear, although I did try. I always thought I was a bit of a snappy dresser, so the following Sunday saw me dressed to kill in my grey pinstriped bell bottoms, brown belt, and Beatle boots to match with zips on the side, and my new pink shirt-and-tie combo. Geez what a looker, the height of 'far-shon' along with my flowing locks of long, blondie brown hair and a shadow of fuzz on my chin. My friends nearly laughed me out of the place as they jeered. They were wearing long shorts, plain shirts and socks pulled up to their knees, so who were they to talk?!

It wasn't long after this that I started walking one of the Anderson sisters home from morning church services. Fran and I were immediately attracted to one another. It would seem the elder sister, Sally, was already spoken for. This was the start of a romance that would last more than thirty-five years.

The former Baptist church, Sandgate

4 | INTERVENTION

We walked, we talked for months, Fran and I became very close and one thing led to another ... we made love which was, to us, a natural progression since we'd both fallen head over heels for one another. It was beautiful, we both felt uplifted by one another—this love thing was a fantastic! An exhilarating emotion, and our hearts felt full, the butterflies never stopped every time we met. We were so enamoured with each other that we felt elevated to an existential plane and love was grand.

Fast-forward a few months to May 1970 and Fran's mother insisted her daughter had a pregnancy test, since her period had stopped. A short, but succinct, visit to Doctor McKeering's surgery in Sandgate was to see the test proved positive. Fran felt a beam of happiness within herself upon hearing this news, but she was brought very quickly down to earth—with a thud—when her mother visibly showed signs of both shock and disappointment. Both women felt a degree of embarrassment in front of their long-time family physician. Dr McKeering probably wasn't surprised nor affected by this turn of events, it happened regularly ... young love.

The short journey home to Nashville by bus was held in a gloomy silence, two sets of eyes looking in opposite directions, staring out of the windows as the suburbs passed slowly by. Not a word was spoken. Heavy contemplation: Fran could not be sure if she was happy for us, or overcome by the humiliation she'd bestowed upon her mother. The air was thick with discomfiture. Even upon arrival at their rented home in Darling Street the mood was never going to elevate. Fran's mother, Emily, who was single, hit the roof. She felt safe to explode now within the confines of her own four walls and questioned how Fran could do this to her? What was she thinking to let such a thing happen? Emily then shuffled off broodingly and retired to her bedroom, and silence prevailed for the rest of the day.

Fran relayed the news to me later that day after work over the phone in hushed tones and although we had a very stilted conversation, we were both quietly ecstatic about our news. It was actually hard to contain our excitement noiselessly. It was becoming patently obvious though that neither of us were quite sure what a storm we had created.

Fran also told me her mother got the information first hand as she was present at the doctor's rooms and was not happy about the situation at all. Shit, shit, shit!! I had to think on my feet here and quickly decided to tell my parents personally sometime later because I didn't want them hearing it from another source. I thought then, as now, that it was pretty brave of me to confront my

4 | INTERVENTION

parents, and on getting the news they did likewise and completely lost the plot. The 'how could you' echoed out as loudly in Fourth Avenue as it had in Nashville several kilometres away. Disappointment formed a cloud over us both separately, so tangible that you could almost touch it.

Moving forward, we were now a little dazed: apart by a couple of suburbs, a little more than confused, happily in love, but extremely naïve. What happened next? We lost complete control of our lives.

The patriarchal system was in full tilt in the '60s and '70s in Australia: men made all the decisions in society and a woman's place was raising children and being in the kitchen as a homemaker. Men sat in judgement about how young men and young (especially pregnant) single women were treated, while women sat by and had no voice, and little influence.

The church intervened quickly and within days a collaboration between both my parents and Fran's mother had begun, and a meeting with the newly appointed pastor of the Baptist Church took place. Fran and I were never invited to attend these meetings even though it was our futures they were discussing. The Sandgate Baptist Church was known for its iconic landmark building by the waterfront in Sandgate which still stands as a poignant reminder of days gone by.

A course of action was decided: the child would be adopted. There was nothing in this conversation that even hinted it was 'our' child, a human being made by love, no less. That notion was summarily brushed aside. There were no *ands*, no *if's*, no *buts*; it was an affirmative decision and a final one at that. This amounted to coercion in the very sense of the word, it was to be a forced adoption, and we were powerless to do anything about what was to come next.

My parents and Fran's mother conformed; they just went along with the authoritarian figure that the pastor was. He must have had orders from above his station (Baptist church management or God himself) or, perhaps, took it upon himself to implement the rules. This was also to be the start of the insidious negativity where Fran was told that she couldn't possibly look after this child, especially an illegitimate child. The start of mutterings that the child would have a better life with other people raising her, people who really cared and could look after a baby 'properly'. The inference heavily weighed against *any* possibility that we could look after a child at all. We were deemed incapable of such care. There was a myriad of excuses piled up against us, especially the social stigma of Fran being unwed and being unfit to be a mother. All of this came along with the exclusivity of shame and guilt too.

The system was the system, rightly or wrongly, and that was that—no one questioned it. The machine had kicked into top gear and the juggernaut had left town. In fact, for our parents this was probably seen as a great resolution, a solution to all of our 'problems', no less.

4 | INTERVENTION

Not one in this quartet had even considered the long-term repercussions of their decisions upon us or our unborn child. We were unwittingly being led into a dystopian future by them and, we too, were blissfully unaware of it. No one ever explained to Fran what her rights might have been or what support may have been available to her. She would be turning eighteen years old by the time our baby was born, but this was summarily dismissed.

We were also, from this point forward, to be kept apart. We were not supposed to see each other at all. My parents never discussed any of this in depth with me personally. The fact that my parents were a closed shop when it came to any conversation about anything tangible probably suited me. I thought it would degenerate very quickly into a huge argument, best to 'keep schtum' (a British colloquialism for keeping quiet or playing your cards close to your chest). There was almost nothing said, and we danced around each other quietly. It was brushed over and that was that. I was no longer able to see Fran, though that had been made abundantly clear.

There was also rumour and inuendo floating about that, as a minor, I could see jail time for getting a young woman pregnant. A whisper here and there of carnal knowledge and a threat to be charged and put away for my crime. It was scaremongering from people who had no stake in our relationship, but who were only too willing to put their spin on a situation that didn't concern them. Typical human behaviour really. Little did they know that the age of consent in Queensland was sixteen years of age. We had both consented. Ha! The best laid plans of mice and men, hey? Love conquers all and all that guff. You'll see what I mean shortly.

The Boys' Brigade, what a wonderful institution for supporting young boys as they grow from childhood into the teenage years and then onto manhood, he says cynically. It was meant to be, in every sense of the word, a Christian organisation set up to encourage young men and boys, and to provide a nurturing environment through its many and varied courses and skills-based programs. I'd been a diligent member of the local brigade at the Sandgate Baptist Church for approximately eight years, and had attended many youth camps and skills-based courses over this time; but one night that was all to change.

The following week I fronted the usual Friday night parade dressed in my unform resplendent with the regalia of badges I'd earnt. There were so many badges from completed tasks and years of service there was barely room for any more on my armband. I loved the fact that I'd achieved so much in such a short time. I took a lot of pride in my uniform, making sure everything was crisp and tidy: shoes shined, lapels straightened, creases ironed, and badges polished with Brasso metal polish to make them gleam. Little did I know what was to come next ...

4 | INTERVENTION

We formed up in the church hall on that fateful Friday night, as was customary, in our squads, standing like tin soldiers to attention as the clock ticked 7 o'clock and start time. The Senior Leaders and Officers faced us at the front, and the older higher-ranking boys formed up with their squads in precise lines across the hall. We all did discipline well.

I was some rows back, none the wiser, standing to attention at the end of a line of ten younger boys that I was in charge of. Proceedings would normally see some announcements made and then we would break off into groups to start on various projects that each squad or boy was involved in. Tonight would be different though, much to my dismay and as I was about to find out. Suddenly the norm, and a part of my world which I loved, was to come crashing down as a call went out, "Lance Corporal Kenward to the front."

I gingerly made my way to the front and stood at attention facing the two senior officers, the two brothers who were in charge, and I quietly speculated what was coming next. Our eyes met, the officers' eyes stern and unwavering with more than a tinge of disappointment in me, I could read that much. My eyes were focused squarely as I waited for the axe to fall, this was not going to have a good outcome, whichever way you looked at it. I didn't have to wait long to find out why I'd been singled out from the group.

In front of the whole squadron of 50-plus young men and

boys they informed me I was to be demoted from my rank and had to hand in my Lance Corporal stripe on the spot. My armful of hard-earnt badges followed next. I was confused as to why they would be castigating me; no one had warned me this was going to occur or of the circumstances under which they could do such a thing. The leaders, on the other hand, had obviously planned this well in advance as counselled by the church pastor or others higher up in The Boys' Brigade command chain. They knew exactly what they were doing.

I was so embarrassed that my face flushed with red, I suddenly felt hot. A feeling of sickness turned in the pit of my stomach and my breath shortened, it was the first inkling of the anxiety which would plague me from this day forward. This was the most humiliating act I had ever been subjected to, and if that wasn't enough, I was then told I was no longer in charge of my squad and to fall back in as a general recruit, rank of private, at the back of the room. Shock set in and sat most uncomfortably with me.

The night continued and I was expected to comply and just carry on normally as if nothing had happened. Not one of the senior officers or staff, who I had had a good relationship with (I thought) since childhood, took me aside to explain what had just transpired. I was left to my own devices and to flounder. Over the course of the night while continuing with our usual brigade activities like knot and rope tying, fitness regimes, etc., my friends took me aside and asked what was going on—the 'whys'

4 | Intervention

were endless, their curiosity piqued.

I was definitely in a state of numbness, I could feel that much in my body, my mind wasn't functioning, things were very muddy. I had no idea what had just occurred to me, but as the senior officers were giving me a very wide berth I surmised very quickly that the only-days-old news of me getting a girl pregnant was what it had come down to. Obviously in the *Code of Conduct* of what *not* to do in The Boys' Brigade, I had hit the jackpot. Here was the patriarchal system in play once again. The rest of the night was ... well ... awkward for everyone, to say the least.

I left that night vowing to never return. For an organisation touting to support young men and boys, they had badly let me down and had crushed me in the process. "You'll do as we say, young man, and there will be no questioning the status quo." Surely there could have been some dialogue with me, and the provision of support mechanisms for what had just happened. But no, that didn't happen at all, and I was left alone to fester. Can you imagine this scenario playing out today? Especially where mental health and people's welfare is paramount and considered such a big-ticket item in modern society! I'd be pretty sure they never had any discourse with my parents over this, and neither did I. Another life-changing moment just swept under the carpet.

So, I was belittled and shamed, basically disgraced,

stripped bare. My sense of pride in myself, and of the uniform I wore, was in tatters. I have to say that nearly fifty-five years later as I write this the anger over my treatment is palpable, I can feel it in every inch of my bones.

Where was the love and compassion from a 'Christian' organisation? Nowhere to be seen, I'm afraid. Let's just say my personal mental health and well-being took a big hit that night but, even so, who cared? No one cared at all. Not one person showed any compassion. This was a definitive point in my young life, I knew from this point on there would be only one person who could look after me —and that was **me,** and fuck the rest of them!

5 | LOSING IT ... BIG TIME

Winter 1970—our family was to take a short vacation at Caloundra's Shelley Beach in a beachside house. The old highset traditional all-timber house was full of rooms and corridors, prior to the building of mega complexes and unit towers. Unfortunately, as it was the off-season and, therefore, cheaper the weather was not great, with storms and rain most days.

My relationship with my mum and dad was at an impasse, but one particular day Dad suggested he and I go for a walk along the beach. Why he would suggest this dumbfounded me as it was blowing a bloody gale outside. We cut across the rocky foreshore onto the surf beach at Kings Beach, the surf was huge with the waves being whipped up by the wind. We didn't talk; I basically followed him in silence.

Dad was a man of few words, and much to my amazement as we approached the raging surf he said, "Go on then," and pointed to the sea. I thought this was a pretty crazy idea, but wanting to appear to please my dad, as always, I did what he asked: took off my shirt and entered the boiling mass of the ocean. The waves were huge, and the white water was being whipped up in a frenzied mess.

Now, I was a pretty good swimmer at the time, having been a member of the Sandgate swimming squad, and had entered and won some competitions. But swimming in amongst this melee was a whole different kettle of fish, more like swimming in a washing machine. A fair way offshore, I looked back from beyond the break bobbing in the water holding myself up doing dogpaddle. I could see Dad walking alone along the beach and questioned myself intently if he had wanted or expected me to die out here. Strange thoughts indeed. Did he want me to not come back? Should I end it here so I could take away his disappointment in me? (Even though he'd never said as much.)

The notions passed through my mind quickly and I knew deep down that I'd caused him a lot of grief, it weighed heavily on my shoulders, heavy enough to push me down. His eldest son, who he'd had the best plans for; he had told me I was going to be a racing driver one day. Yes, I thought that it would please him for me to be no more. Suicide seemed like a good option, and it was staring me down.

Time seemed to stand still, momentarily everything became quiet. The sky was dark with heavy cloud, a monochrome look to it, the waves were pounding my body in a regular rhythm, the wind was still raging, my heart was racing out of control. I could have easily ducked beneath the next wave and said goodbye. I

5 | Losing It ... Big Time

actually imagined myself being washed up on the shore. Limp. Dead. But, for some reason I didn't succumb to the urge, and I'm still here, maybe to tell you *this* story.

Fran and I continued to see each other sporadically throughout her early pregnancy and while she was still at home. Although thinking about it now, I'm baffled how we managed it as there were no mobile phones, no internet, or any such other communication device. Although it was long winded, we did have a system of communicating through friends and the like, so no one was ever going to stop us from having contact, however small.

One particular Sunday night, at about the four-month mark, I attended church on the off-chance Fran may be there. She was, so we hand signalled each other to meet around the back of the church. We met up for a few short minutes in the dark shadows and talked briefly before one of the church elders spotted us. All I wanted to do was to check on her well-being, and nothing more, as a few weeks had passed since we had last spoken.

It degenerated into something akin to a military operation. People from the congregation got between us to form a shield, Fran was whisked away into an awaiting car that had the engine running and doors open. How dramatic! All the while I was left on my lonesome looking like an outcast from society, feeling rejected, and having no worth. If it had been back in biblical times, I might have been subject to a stoning to death. Damn those Christians!!

You could feel the tension, see the look of pleasure on the faces of the people as they dispersed after a job well done, a definitive attitude of 'let's wipe our hands of this rebellious young man'. I can't help but be sceptical here. Christian values, hey …

Where was the sympathy, the empathy, support from the people I'd known all my life in this enclave? These people had known me since childhood. It was non-existent, and as cold and as dark as the night itself. It never ceases to amaze me how ordinary people will take sides and not actually think for themselves. Not one person in that congregation stepped up to ask me if I was alright, and I was really a long, long way from okay. With the weight of our situation, I was becoming a very, very angry young man.

The pastor appeared from somewhere, and from a distance—and with authority in his voice—told me I should go home. His audacity meant I saw RED … so I ended up confronting him in all his righteousness, right in his face and marching him backwards out onto Flinders Parade as my feet hit the bitumen underfoot. I was extremely agitated, and he was on the receiving end of my wrath. There were a lot of pent-up emotions bubbling to the surface.

I screamed at him, spitting fire, that I just needed to check how Fran was going, that was all. Why could he

5 | Losing It ... Big Time

not see this? Even in my frantic state of mind I was showing someone (Fran), another human being compassion. But here we had a man of the cloth, a religious—apparently pious—man showing me no compassion whatsoever. All I was getting from him were proverbs and platitudes, and it was confusing.

I had my right fist clenched so hard behind my back that I could feel my nails digging into the flesh of my palm. Tension filled the air; I wanted so much to land one straight on his mush. Suddenly I felt a hand get hold of my right arm pulling me strongly away—it was my mother. I'm not sure if that stopped me but I wish I had hit him even to this day. I think it would have felt pretty good. The consequences may not have been but, hey-ho, sometimes you just 'got to do what you got to do'. It would have been administration of my own form of justice.

In my eyes he was the single person most responsible for creating all of our problems, he was the one who ultimately was making us give our child away. He was playing God, and he was caught in the crossfire of my rage.

A few months later the pastor's very much underaged fifteen-year-old daughter was also found to be pregnant. How ironic, and what a twist of fate. It's amazing how people can be led to believe one story for one scenario, and another if it concerns *their* family. Felt like a double standard to me, still does. The pastor's daughter had her child and kept it. The young couple was supported throughout the pregnancy, and they eventually married.

She was never going to be sent away or shunned by the congregation. What an angel. She was never shamed like we were. She was shown mercy and love and support from all quarters. Why didn't we warrant the same treatment? How contradictory is this? What Christian values are these? In the meantime, I only became more jaded. My trust for anyone was out the window.

Some months after my sixteenth birthday I started an apprenticeship as a fitter-and-turner at the same engineering company in Geebung, on the northside of Brisbane, I'd done holiday work at. It was different this time around though, and I was getting a little more serious money than just a bit of holiday cash. I actually hated it because I wanted to be a signwriter, having developed a flair for drawing. But signwriting was a hard profession to get into in our area since most companies were family owned; hence the sons would be taken on as apprentices first. So, getting a trade under my belt was to become priority number one.

Apprentices back in the '70s were not only considered cheap labour, but generally as dumb bastards too, so to me I'd found a place to sort of fit in. Dad had made enquiries with the management and secured the job for me. So, I was indentured for five years, which included attending regular TAFE college courses at night.

5 | Losing It ... Big Time

Apprenticeships were usually four-year terms but, since my high school year ten results weren't considered so great, I had another year tacked onto my term.

It also went a long way that I'd worked there previously on school holidays, so I had a good feel for the place and knew how things worked, and people knew me. I didn't like the fact that I'd be tied down to this godforsaken place for that long—it seemed like a lifetime. At the time I couldn't see any value in becoming a qualified tradesman either.

I hated the noise, the atmosphere, the work, the smell ... nothing pleased me about working, with the exception of collecting a weekly cash pay packet of $11, which was delivered to your machine personally by the pay clerk each Friday. I'd open that small brown packet and look down at the crisp new notes inside and rattle the change. I was perhaps momentarily dreaming of better things than work and what I could spend my money on.

My vinyl record collection was starting to expand with the likes of Led Zeppelin, Jethro Tull, and Pink Floyd. I had bought, on lay-by, a small stereo unit with a turntable and twin speakers from the Chandlers store in Sandgate. Buying records was a treat as the store had rows of new releases set out, all the latest and greatest hits by bands from all over the world. There was also a booth where you could ask the shop assistant to play your selected record through a set of headphones. She would even ask if there was a particular track you'd like to listen to before buying the record. Great times! Records were cheap, shop assistants had time to serve you, the music really was a way to escape from reality. Still is.

6 | Staying Connected

Part of our plan was to stay in touch and stay connected. Nobody was going to come between Fran and me, and the more they tried the more we strengthened our resolve to stay together. Bugger every last one of them!

I used to tell my mother I was going out to see a mate in Brighton, one of the neighbouring suburbs to Sandgate, when I was actually going to see Fran in Nashville which was close by too.

I'd ride my pushbike for stealth. Nice and quiet, pushbikes. It was approaching winter in Brisbane and already quite cool, especially when exposed to the wind. But I'd rug up and take off at one hundred miles per hour up the road.

The plan was to meet at Fran's house, I'd park my bike at the back, jump the low chain wire fence and creep covertly towards the back of the house. Fortunately, Fran's bedroom was right at the back of the house, and I could see the light on through the narrow back window. I'd wait, and then wait some more, hoping I hadn't been noticed by the neighbours either side, then Fran would open the window to see if I was there.

She'd signal for me to come up—coast clear, as it were.

This was easier said than done as her bedroom's window sill was at least three metres off the ground. Never one to be foiled by obstacles, I'd quietly move the metal garbage can from nearby and stand on top of it. Maintaining my balance, I'd then get a handhold on the window sill and climb up with my feet scrambling against the timber plank wall-sheeting, quietly, ssshhh! The window was a single casement-style timber framed pane of ornamental glass which opened outwards, and I'd shimmy through the narrow gap as quietly as possible. Sometimes I'd get a bit stuck and have my legs flailing outside the house while my top half struggled inside, while trying not to laugh hysterically. All this while Fran's mother was in the next room or down the corridor. At all times I felt like a ninja creeping about on tip-toes.

Fran, August 1970

Once inside it was down to whispers to talk. We'd sit on the bed and chat away about how our weeks had been, ever so quietly, and listen for any movement from her mother. At this point Fran was still gainfully employed as a dental assistant at Toombul Shoppingtown, but her employment was soon to come to an embarrassing end since she was starting to expand around the waistline. She would shortly be leaving home too—disgraced and shamed.

Fran's mother may have had suspicions that something was going on in the bedroom next door to her room, as

6 | Staying Connected

on occasions something would get knocked or moved, unfamiliar sounds, creaking floorboards and the like during our dalliances. We jokingly coined Fran's mum 'Mrs Clippety Cloppety' as she used to walk about the house in heavy shoes. Sometimes I suspect she may have known I was there all along and put the formal shoes on purposely. I mean, who walks around inside the house with formal shoes on? I shudder to think what would have happened had she actually found me in there.

Me, August 1970

One such night, with our senses always on alert, we heard her mother making her way back down the corridor from the kitchen, but she stopped short of turning into her bedroom ... a short silence ... then there was a knock on the door. I moved hastily and slid quickly under the bed, fortunately it was one of the old-fashioned beds which stood a long way off the floor. Thank God for the clearance under it as there was certainly no cupboard space to hide in! Fran's mother just wanted to say goodnight and give her a hug (and probably check if I was in fact there). In the meantime, I was backed in against the wall, breathing slowly, looking at the two pins which were her mother's legs within touching distance from me. A scary moment, but I was not discovered. Luckily, even though it was a bit dusty under the bed I didn't sneeze!!

As always, our meetups were very short. Leaving a little

while later I'd have to squeeze quietly back out through the narrow window (feet first) again and try not to knock over the bin on my way back down. With the bin reinstalled in its rightful place I'd then crouch down low and run really fast to where my push bike was stashed to ensure I wouldn't be seen, especially by the nearby residents.

This whole process of meeting up was fraught with hazards. One night, on my pushbike ride home, I was in a bit of a rush and was steaming down a hill entering Sandgate's town precinct. I was head down and tail up as I hit a huge rut in the road. Next thing I knew the front wheel dug in and I was flung over the handlebars and crashing totally out of control. The landing was rather ungracious as my hands, elbows, and knees got skinned in the process. That really hurt and there was blood pouring out of me from all corners. I limped home to ride another day as I couldn't care less what happened to me physically in the process of keeping our love alive.

Around four months into her pregnancy Fran was starting to 'show', so she was sent to a Salvation Army home. There was a Matron in charge of the building, and she was a gruff character to say the very least.

The house Fran was banished to was a very large and imposing building in the old Queenslander style, located on Stanley Street in South Brisbane. It was quite near to the Brisbane River, and the newly-built Victoria Bridge. This was a seedy part of Brisbane known for its old

6 | Staying Connected

boarding houses and cheap squat accommodation. The Queensland Cultural Centre, Art Gallery, and Museum now stand in its place.

It looked like it had had many alterations and extensions during its long life, due to the discoloured fibro wall sheeting, different coloured wall panels, and the corrugated roof sheeting's rusty appearance. It had a verandah on the upper level, louvered windows all around and it nestled in a small, badly maintained yard close to an industrial area. It also backed onto the rear of a service station which, in itself was to provide some entertainment when a gas tank blew up. The explosion was huge and the fireball from it singed anything nearby.

There was no signage on the outside entry to distinguish it as a home to young single pregnant mothers-to-be, or that it was also a refuge to those in need of short-term shelter from marriage breakups and the like. Never was the old adage, 'If these walls could talk, the tales they could tell', more true. The inside of the house looked like it was badly in need of a coat of paint, the furnishings were sparse and not many pieces matched each other. The odd painting decorated the walls, but just like the residents, none were masterpieces, and it was quite an odd collection.

The upstairs quarters were the sole realm of those individuals who had been involved in some sort of calamity in their lives; most were there short term, some were young, some were old, and some were children, but all were seeking a safe haven from the ills of the world. Nevertheless, all were happy to have a roof over their heads.

The six or so staff under the command of the Head Matron also wore the crisp white uniforms with epaulets on the shoulders and badges to show their rank, and that they were proud members of the Salvation Army; they were always well presented and their uniforms neatly pressed. They were not residents of the house and merely performed their daily tasks to return home after their shift.

The downstairs area of the house was reserved for a constant stream of young single mothers-to-be who were here to be hidden from the world's gaze. It consisted of a small front entry off which led a long corridor to the rear of the premises. Either side of the hallway was a rather large lounge, a sitting room, a dining area, and at the rear a kitchen. Rearwards of the kitchen there was a small verandah which led to the backyard and clothes line, and opposite this yet another room in the maze which was to become home to Fran for the next five months.

Her room was dark and dingy; the only natural light streamed through a small row of louvered windows just below ceiling level. It served to highlight the lack of opulence of the room even more. Four single steel-framed beds occupied the floor, each with a side table and a hanging cupboard opposite, a solitary light bulb

6 | Staying Connected

hung centrally on its cord from the discoloured nine-foot-high patchwork ceiling. Even it looked lonely.

In a twist of fate this home had also provided a refuge for Fran's mother many years previously to escape the battering she was receiving at the hand of her drunken husband. He was once a good man and a hard worker, happy to support his little family, though that would change with the advent of World War II in Europe.

As a young man he was drafted into the Australian Air Force. His service in the RAAF as a Lancaster bomber pilot would see him stationed in England, flying dozens of bombing raids over Germany. He was also later stationed in Burma and Singapore for a time, and he reached the rank of Warrant Officer. He returned some years later a broken man having lost a lot of his flight crew and mates during his bombing missions.

By weight of numbers and losses throughout the war he was lucky to be alive and to have made it through. The atrocities of war and the horrific scenes he had witnessed affected him greatly, so his medicine of choice, and his undoing, were to be found at the bottom of a bottle of alcohol. He lived a solitary life on Macleay Island off the coast of Brisbane in his later years, estranged to the Anderson family. The only time I met him he got roaring drunk on one glass of beer, and we never saw him again.

Fran would be boarding at the Salvation Army home, and earning her keep, for the term of her pregnancy. Over the next five months she was involved in the endless duties of cleaning, washing, ironing, and cooking under the guidance of Salvation Army personnel—there was very little idle time. Fran made a friend in a rather large woman who worked in the kitchen, and together through laughter they tried their best to make light of the conundrum they found themselves in.

There were rules to be followed, procedures in place, and timetables. The day started promptly with a mass breakfast sitting for all residents at 7 a.m., and every morning the menu choice was minimal. A pervasive 9 p.m. curfew made sure the residents knew their place in life as it now was. There were often complaints from those huddled around the single television in the lounge, as 9 p.m. was considered prime viewing time. There was almost a code of silence between the unmarried mothers here, the feeling fostered that they were here because they were disgraced in the eyes of society. Stigmatised to know thy place!

This shift in location made it somewhat harder for us to see each other, but we did arrange some short liaisons at the Victoria Bridge at the top of the city. I'd take the train into the city while Fran waddled slowly across the bridge. It would seem odd nowadays for a single young pregnant woman to be walking around alone in the streets of a city, in any city, but walk she did. No one ever questioned Fran's disappearance from the home at

6 | Staying Connected

night either.

We'd walk around the city shops at the top end of town for a while holding hands tightly, gazing into the brightly lit shopfront displays, looking at glitzy material things on offer that we couldn't afford. We felt like a couple of paupers, and it was probably true.

We'd then come to rest and sit in a bus shelter nearby watching the river beneath us, the constant flow of the river reminding us of the flow of our lives now. Ever moving, ever changing, never static.

Time was tight, but it was a time for us to reinforce our love for one another. We were conscious of not wanting to be seen in public by any of the staff from the 'Salvo' home as this may have caused us yet more trouble. I saw it as my duty to support Fran above all else, and I loved the feeling of our baby moving under my hand as we cuddled. The three of us were connected, there was no doubt even if the world around us was trying it's darndest to make it otherwise.

We'd trundle back across the Victoria Bridge making sure we were out of sight of the home before saying our goodbyes. Walking back across the bridge alone I'd often come across old guys, street beggars asking for money. I had none to give, my pockets were empty as was my mind; at sixteen I was emotionally and physically depleted and the weight was starting to feel heavy.

The clock was ever ticking, we basically had no plan for

ourselves and our child's wellbeing, it was a day-to-day existence, and it seemed Fran was getting bigger every time we met up.

As part of trying to save ourselves and our child from our coming fate I decided to contact Pastor Maxwell Howard in Gordon Park, his new enclave. He'd been the previous minister at Sandgate Baptist for many years before moving onto another area. I'd known Mr Howard for all of my life, he was always a gentle and caring man, so I rang him one night from a public phone box to put our plight to him. My expectations were high, surely Mr Howard would know what to do, he'd know how to fix this or at least have options to discuss.

But as it turned out, it was an all too short phone call as once I explained our circumstances he cut me short and said there was nothing he could do because it was out of his jurisdiction! I had basically just been stonewalled by a man whom I thought I could trust, but as it turned out Pastor Maxwell Howard was in the ranks of those who toed the church's party line. There would be no help from any quarter, the muddle we were in was to continue as just that.

I replaced the handset on the public telephone, bewildered that yet another avenue was closed to us. The sound of the remaining coins being ejected from the coin holder only serving to bring my attention back to my present reality—no one was going to save us.

7 | Birth Days

Early September 1970, Fran had turned eighteen years old the previous month, and her waistline was expanding exponentially. She was really starting to show, and it was hard to hide the fact that she was now nearly seven months pregnant. She had been coming back to Nashville, near Sandgate, from the Salvation Army Home on a fortnightly basis to visit her mother and stay overnight. There was no fanfare, no celebrations on her eighteenth. Fran's mother often made jibes at her during these visits, reinforcing the fact that she'd *ruined her life* ... as if we didn't know that. It was being drummed in pretty hard.

Fran would catch the train to Sandgate and then catch a bus for her onward journey of five kilometres to the suburbs. This gave us a window of opportunity to meet up, albeit for the shortest possible time. Sometimes she'd delay the trip on the first bus just so we'd have a few more minutes together and catch the next. I don't think her mum was any the wiser, we figured trains and buses always ran late. My parents also had no idea where I was or what I was doing, nor cared less I suspect.

One Saturday morning Fran arrived in Sandgate for a

weekend reprieve from the hostel in South Brisbane. We met at the station and walked the shortish distance to the Sandgate waterfront to sit on a park bench to chat and catchup. From the get-go I could tell Fran's whole demeanour had changed, it seemed her usually joyful mood—on seeing me—now had a cloud hanging over it. She was far from happy about how her life was panning out. She'd felt rejected and unsupported and felt the full brunt of being hidden away from society for her mistakes.

There was very little joy to be had from her (our) situation and I couldn't be sure whether I was helping or hindering either. It was a confusing time for both of us. As we sat gazing out over the expanse of Moreton Bay on that clear, cool morning, the blue sky above framed the sunlit islands in the distance, their white sandhills standing out across the expanse of water making a picturesque backdrop. Little did we know then that those islands would provide a home and family for our unborn child to grow up in.

Our short, sharp visits would continue until Tuesday, the 10th of November 1970. At around 6 p.m. I waited at the Sandgate station as the train pulled in. Fran did not alight as per usual. *It'll be okay, she'll be on the next one.* She wasn't, nor the next one, nor the next one. Something must have happened—she was never this late. We had always met up on those Tuesdays and I was starting to get worried; a sense of dread was starting to overtake me. We had no way to communicate so it was

7 | BIRTH DAYS

all a guess where she might be.

Having waited patiently for two hours, at round 8 p.m. I decided to ring the Salvation Army home in South Brisbane from a pay phone close by to check if Fran had left for the day or was still in residence. The answer I got from the stranger on the other end almost collapsed my legs out from under me. She had been taken to Boothville House in Windsor to have the baby early that morning. My mind was muddled, and I couldn't think straight. How many hours ago? What was I supposed to do now? The question hung in the air as cold as a winter's night.

How could I have not known? Why did no one tell me? The anxiety I was feeling was overtaking me and I paced relentlessly. How could I have not been with Fran to support her? Did she even know I was standing here at Sandgate waiting for her? But wait a minute, this wasn't about me was it. Was her family with her, did they even know she'd just given birth? Was she okay, was my baby okay? So many emotions and I didn't know where to direct them. What was the right thing to do now? I had no idea what was going on or which way to turn, and I had no one to talk to.

Fran had arisen early that morning after a restless sleep the night before. We'd met in the city the previous night at the Victoria Bridge for a short time and Fran seemed to have boundless energy, more than at any previous time. Something had started changing, moving on as she just wanted to walk and walk energetically which was surprising as she looked so expansive. Back at the hostel she started feeling tummy cramps through the night. Then, as Mother Nature took over, her waters broke soon afterwards. She had no idea what was going on or what to expect, so she stayed in the wet bed with her nightie hitched up on her knees and called for help.

Realising what was happening the Matron quickly called a Yellow Cab, but not before berating Fran for making such a mess of 'her' bed linen. Only minutes passed before the taxi arrived, and the driver, a swarthy Italian man, looked pretty startled when he found out his new fare was a young woman on the verge of giving birth. He wasn't overly happy, and he drove his orange four-door Falcon XD sedan like a maniac, dodging and weaving wildly in peak hour traffic through the Brisbane city streets on the nearly eight-kilometre drive north to Windsor and Boothville Mother's Hospital. Fran wasn't sure whether she should be more worried by the regular contractions she was experiencing, or if she would actually arrive at her destination in one piece.

Passing through the gates and making his way up the crushed stone driveway to the circular car park near the front entrance, the driver passed a huge sigh of relief as he certainly didn't want to have to deal with helping to birth a newborn in the back seat of his cab. That could have made—or ruined—his whole day.

7 | Birth Days

It was 7:30 a.m. as Fran was guided into the birthing suite; as she changed into a standard issue gown, she could scarcely believe the intensity and the loneliness of this cold institution. She'd spend the day in hours of hard labour assisted by Dr Elliot.

By 12:30 p.m. Fran had spent a lot of time alone between the nurse's check-ups, having to deal with the sporadic pain while contemplating the four stark white walls before her. Soon Dr Elliott returned along with a midwife, this was to be the crowning moment. He started by instructing Fran to bear down, as she was fully dilated and well ready to begin the birthing process. It was a completely natural birth causing tears in Fran's nether regions as she brought our baby into the world. At 1:25 p.m. Baby Anderson saw the light of day for the first time.

Fran's mother and eldest sister had been called sometime that day to attend, but waited in a lounge elsewhere in the building during the labour. Later, back in the stark ward Fran was shown to the shower, she spent an age in that room feeling the warmth of the hot water trickling over her now worn-out body. She wasn't in any hurry to face the world after her ordeal. Afterwards she was shown her bed, she climbed in and felt the sheets starched stiff and heavy, even the bed felt uninviting.

Her mother was asked in and asked Fran if she was okay. Fran wasn't quite sure what she had meant by that.

Alright how? Mentally? Physically? I've just given birth, surely to God you know what that feels like, Mother?

As for me, shock was taking over; even walking was difficult, and it had become a chore just to put one foot in front of the other. I had no idea how to deal with what was happening to me: this daze, shivers coursing through me—I could feel it in my body, such an uneasiness and a clouded mind.

After walking the streets for some time—to find some semblance of calm—I went home. Mum asked me where I'd been, I concocted some cock-and-bull story about being out with mates. But also added a passing comment that Fran had had the baby. I made my way clumsily to my room at the front of the house feeling light-headed and stunned, still anxious.

Mum didn't notice anything was wrong, she was oblivious to it all. She'd had my dinner on a slow heat in the oven and brought it into my room on a tray. She then asked me quite nonchalantly for some details about the baby.

"Boy or girl?" she asked brightly. I told her I knew nothing other than a baby had been born that morning, I had no idea where or even when. And in a rage, overcome with emotion, I yelled at her that I didn't want that muck on the plate!! She left taking the tray with her and I smashed my fist right through a glass panelled door—the exasperation, the pain, the hurt, the confusion kept on coming in waves. I was a mess physically, and destroyed

7 | Birth Days

emotionally. I couldn't cry; I must have been suppressing the tears then because they just wouldn't come. Tears may have helped to ease my feelings, if only they had come. I was so unsettled and unnerved that night that sleep evaded me as well.

I lay awake for hours going over all the possibilities that today had brought to the fore, none more so than that Fran was alone, somewhere in a hospital. I also knew that Dad would be coming home later off night shift to receive the news. In the absolute crisis scenario that was going on in my head I envisaged him getting this latest information from Mum and then coming into my room to give me a damned good belting. Later I overheard Mum and Dad talking in the kitchen in muffled tones as I lay in bed scared to death, shaking. Fortunately, nothing eventuated. Nothing was ever said either ... the quiet was disconcerting and home did not feel safe.

In the following days I fronted up at work as usual, then one day during a smoko break I phoned Boothville Mother's Hospital from a nearby pay phone and asked what the visiting hours were—at least I knew that much. I knew I wasn't supposed to see Fran, or my child, but I thought, *Let them try and stop me!* I was going to see her by hook or by crook, so I hatched a plan.

The next few days were fraught with uncertainty, I didn't know which way to turn, and there was no one to ask advice from, no one. I kept on going to work every day but just kept to myself; at night I'd confine myself to my room at home or spend as little time as possible there. Time was ticking away, and Fran was ensconced at Boothville for at least a week, so I had to pick my time to visit.

All the time my head was battling with scenarios: should I visit? Shouldn't I visit? My responsibility was to back Fran here, but how? I really had no idea what to do and I'd been procrastinating badly for days. If I decided to see Fran, would I be challenged by someone in authority? Just like every other decision we'd tried in vain to make prior to now. The last thing I wanted to do was to bring Fran any more strife or have a confrontation with family members.

8 | THE VISIT TO BOOTHVILLE

Day eight: Tuesday, the 17th of November 1970. I thought, *Bugger the consequences and bugger everyone else!* I caught the train to Fortitude Valley station early in the evening and walked the five kilometres uphill and down dale to the hospital. On arrival at 43 Seventh Avenue, Windsor, the imposing two-storey form of Boothville House confronted me. This unique, vintage building stood tall and dimly lit on a large, sloping, tree-lined block. Imposing and uninviting.

I actually felt sick to the pit of my stomach knowing that Fran and my child were inside as I made my way up the gravel drive at a clip and with purpose. With my senses heightened I could hear the gravel crunching loudly beneath my feet. I walked more gingerly the closer I got to the house, not knowing what sort of reception I'd get from the staff or from Fran. I approached the circular driveway lined with flower gardens, which led to an ornate covered walkway area and made my way up the six or seven front stairs onto the veranda. My feet now felt like lead, but I dragged them across to the front doors ... heavy, man, heavy.

My heart was beating out of my chest; I then let myself in through the huge glass-panelled double doors. They were painted maroon with large, polished brass handles, they weren't locked. This led me into an open area and foyer, and I wasn't challenged by anyone ... yet. There was no one in attendance as far as I could see. The place was deadly silent, old, vintage, it smelt antiseptic and the aroma hung in the air. A dimly lit ornate chandelier hung centrally over a wide stairway draped with a dark red carpet-runner down its centre. Brass stair-rods glistened across the width of each step. Beautifully polished timber handrails curved and followed the stairs down each side.

Boothville Mothers' Hospital, Windsor

I found someone passing by, one of the other patients, and asked where Fran was situated, and I was directed to the staircase leading to the upper floors. When I reached the landing, I was confronted with an illuminated sign to my right indicating 'Nursery'. The

8 | THE VISIT TO BOOTHVILLE

walls stood silent with a starkness of drab white paint and a layer of green and red flower-patterned wallpaper below a polished timber dado rail. Lonely light bulbs hung from the ceiling emitting an eerie glow.

As I passed slowly by, the doors of the nursery were closed and beyond the glass panels I could see several cribs lined up, babies wrapped tightly in swaddling. My baby was in there, I knew it. At this point I didn't know if I had a son or a daughter, but one way or another I was about to find out.

I found Fran in the next room; it was as oppressive and drab-looking as the rest of the place. In this restrictive and sterile environment, it felt like the walls were closing in on its residents. The room's high ceilings looked down on the six or seven beds which took up the spaces around the perimeter; most of them had curtains pulled around them providing some privacy for the occupants. Single lightbulbs hung over each pod providing a stark glow. We hugged tentatively, so happy to be reunited but ever so mindful of who may be watching us—or me in particular.

Fran took me back to where her bed was and we stood awkwardly talking. She filled me in that we had a beautiful baby daughter and that she was doing well. She was a good weight (7lb 15oz) and looked delightful too. Fran had named her Priscilla, just as we had previously discussed. Fran told me when she was born our baby didn't cry, not even a whimper. It was only when the doctor turned her upside down to smack her on the bum that she yelped. She soon settled back down though, and was calm. I was filled with pride that our love had produced a beautiful child, my daughter, our daughter. It made me feel really good ... all but momentarily.

During the previous few days Fran had also been subjected to the now familiar line from the staff who reiterated the fact that giving up her baby was the best thing she could do for the welfare of the child. She'd have a better life than we could possibly give her with folk who would look after her 'properly'. The well-worn inference was that we couldn't feasibly look after a baby at all ... really? I mean, really, were they *so* sure of that?! Nonetheless it was the party line they pushed.

During her internment one of the senior staff members told Fran the only thing that may bring the wheels of the adoption process grinding to a halt was if the child had any 'faults', big or small. The same staff member had brought Baby Anderson out to see Fran early that week and pronounced, "You can't give this child up you know — look at her, she's cross-eyed!" What a revelation, Fran said nothing being too stunned to reply, but secretly hoped it to be true. It must have been a momentary imperfection of a newborn finding her sight, as later in the week no such flaw was found.

For the first time since we'd met I noticed Fran looked really drained and very fragile, and I learned she'd cried

8 | THE VISIT TO BOOTHVILLE

a bucketful of tears over the past few days. Our conversation was fraught and hurried since we both knew, in the scheme of things, I wasn't supposed to be there, and if found out I could be given my marching orders by the Salvation Army staff at any time.

To say Fran was a little cool towards me would be an understatement. I wasn't particularly surprised by this as she'd had a week of recovery trying to get over giving birth and the damage it had done to her body, let alone the anguish of other people's decisions weighing heavily on her life. She felt just as alone and abandoned as I did, or even more so.

I wasn't allowed to see my daughter, there was no way that was possible (apparently). Should I have insisted on seeing my child? Could I have insisted on seeing my child? Maybe I could have if I had been game enough to push the envelope with the hospital staff. But then there were always the unknowns: would the staff have pushed back about me actually being there? Or maybe I would have found that one sympathetic nurse who might have said yes. I often wonder the IFs. If I had seen my child through that window, how would I have reacted? Would I have fought harder and gone hammer-and-tong to keep her? Might that have changed my view on this whole situation and seen me push for other options to keep our baby? I think I might have been pushing shit uphill, who knows, as it never happened.

It was a sad, sad day especially when Fran told me she

had signed the adoption papers (*Form 1 Queensland The Adoption of Children Acts 1964 to 1965 Form of General Consent by Parent or Guardian to Adoption Order*) the day before — the 16th of November 1970 — and our daughter would be leaving within days to be relocated to her new family.

When she was confronted by a staff member with the adoption order Fran had asked for 'someone' (presumably me, or her mother, or her sisters) to be present before signing the papers. The nurse had most blandly replied, "It's simple—just sign them." Fran's last-ditch effort to get a reprieve hadn't worked, there was no way to get out of this conundrum. Feeling coerced and pressured she reluctantly signed the papers. Even though she was over eighteen years of age she just did as she was instructed, no one ever told her what her rights were.

The weight of this action brought emotions to the fore that felt foreign and wrong, and once again opened the flood gates. Fran found a place to hide, curled up on the floor with her knees drawn to her chest behind a drape of curtains—no longer able or willing to face the enormity of what had just occurred.

We had also briefly discussed the other patients interned in that room and other mothers elsewhere in the expansive upper floors within Boothville. Most women in this wing were single girls in the same position as Fran, and they had all intimately discussed their

8 | THE VISIT TO BOOTHVILLE

personal dilemmas across the room. The young women came from diverse backgrounds and towns across Queensland and had different stories to tell as to how they had arrived here. There was a mixture of healthy boy and girl babies born to them, and one of the girls had given birth to twins who were subsequently put up for adoption as well. I don't know if those twins were kept together or separated—either way it was heart wrenching for all concerned.

The system would see them all tarred with the same brush though. You were here because you had done something wrong in the eyes of certain people in society. You were also to be dealt with in the manner prescribed by that society's rules.

The Boothville Hospital building was built between 1887 and 1900 and was then known as *Monte Video*. It is considered a villa-style building and was heritage listed in 1992. It was run by the Salvation Army and had a general maternity ward and another for young single mothers who were going to be adopting their babies. These babies were considered to be born out of wedlock or illegitimate.

All the single mothers there were given no other option but to give their babies up for adoption. They had all had the adoption papers put under their noses in the days straight after giving birth to their children. This deliberate act was more than likely designed to catch the young women at their most vulnerable, and so there was no recourse to change their minds or be influenced by outsiders in any way. It was a system; no one who entered this establishment under these circumstances could challenge the status quo—once you were within the matrix.

No one ever told Fran what her rights were. Never in a million years would Fran have given up our child if she had been aware of her civil or human rights. She would have been fully justified to keep our child without anyone else's consent—she just didn't know it.

I'm sure the minister of the church would have known these facts, but it seems he chose not to disclose this to Fran. I believe his one and only agenda was 'adoption at all costs'.

Fran's mother, and Fran's four sisters, *all* saw our baby before the adoption, but they all said nothing. They knew how old Fran was too, and may have been aware of her rights. But, once again, no one said a thing.

I was livid finding this out in 2025, and it produced exactly the same emotions I felt fifty-five years earlier: anger, frustration, disappointment, anxiety—to name but a few. It never leaves you … it's totally fucked.

At Boothville, *how* paperwork was completed may have been totally dependent on who was in charge or on duty on that shift, and which way their ethics leaned. If the

8 | THE VISIT TO BOOTHVILLE

duty nurse or sister was sympathetic, they might be a little kinder and show some compassion and fill the paperwork in correctly. If you dealt with the Matron or head nurse things may have been looked upon differently or more indirectly. There was, perhaps, a chance here for those in charge to manipulate the paperwork, thereby making it harder to trace any given child's record of birth in future.

There were also glitches in the system, as Fran would find out much to her dismay. At some point during the week, Baby Anderson was brought out for Fran to bottle feed. Fran thought this odd, but quite happily proceeded to give our baby the bottle anyway. It was lovely to hold her, our child was placid and rarely cried, and she looked happy to have arrived into the world.

It didn't take long for a staff member to realise her mistake and return and snatch the baby away again saying she didn't realise Fran wasn't keeping her. It may be difficult to comprehend, but there was to be no bonding allowed between mothers and their newborns at any point if the adoption order was in place. The rules were in place and were not to be broken. The cruelty of this is substantial. Another one of the 'inmates' was actually assigned to look after our baby for feeds, nappy changing, and the like. She reported to Fran that our baby was doing well and commented how much she looked like her father, as she had seen me during my visit.

I felt heartbroken and there was nothing I could do, not a thing. I was totally non-existent in this environment, a non-entity, *persona non grata* according to the 'authorities'.

One of Fran's older sisters turned up with her husband, surprising us and cutting our visit incredibly short. They acknowledged me and I acknowledged them in return; there weren't any bad feelings shown toward me as far as I could tell, but things were definitely a bit frosty. I was guessing that they probably hated me as much as everyone else did, and had every right to as well. I will admit though, I did have a feeling of being on edge the whole time I was there, and I felt some relief at someone else attending the bedside with Fran as it masked my presence there.

Fran's sister and brother-in-law did, however, get to see our baby in the nursery during the visit. They weren't gone for long and when they returned said nothing about how Baby Anderson looked, not to me at least. There were none of the normal congratulatory remarks or pats on the back, there was just more of the *uncomfortable*.

The end of visiting hours came all too soon, and it was then—as another surprise—that I found out Fran was going home. It was the very reason her sister and brother-in-law had come. This left me in a precarious position, what the hell was I supposed to do now? I felt like I was in the way ... again ... as always!

Fran packed what small amount of clothing she had with

8 | THE VISIT TO BOOTHVILLE

her into a carry bag and got changed. The visit was short and bittersweet, and as I went to leave, I kissed Fran goodbye and gave her an awkward hug that was far too short and said, "See you soon." I was hopeful of that small fact but who knew, certainly neither of us knew what was to come next. The whole of our lives seemed a mystery at this point.

As we walked out of the room I glanced to my left and stole a look through the nursery doors. The cribs positions had been changed around from my earlier glimpse as some had been moved out to see their mothers or carers for feeds or changing nappies, etc. In what felt like a time warp—in the nanoseconds available—I looked all but hopelessly for an identification tag for Baby Anderson, my daughter. She was in there somewhere; I just couldn't find her.

As we said our goodbyes at the front of Boothville, Fran's brother-in-law, Ian, surprisingly offered me a lift home. I gladly accepted, and was quite taken back by this small act of kindness since there had been zero kindness shown to me by anyone lately, or at least that's what I perceived. Sitting in the back seat as the car made its way slowly down the gravel driveway we both looked back over our shoulders to the dim lights of Boothville disappearing behind us. We then looked at each other with tears forming in our eyes, we didn't have to say a word, we both knew exactly what we were leaving behind.

On the way back to Sandgate Fran and I held hands across the back seat in the car, she was definitely on her side of the car pressed up against the door, almost coiled up. I was sitting on my side, and although we weren't far apart physically, the distance felt like a mile, a yawning chasm. There was an uneasiness to the whole situation, and you could almost cut the air with a knife. Travelling through the northern suburbs of Brisbane in the Morris 1100 the conversation was a little stilted at first, but fortunately we found common ground once we got onto our mutual interest in music which put me, and them I suspect, a little more at ease.

I asked them to drop me off at the top of Fourth Avenue in Sandgate near the shops, a short walk from home. I leaned across to kiss Fran goodbye and not much else was said. What could you say? I knew though that I needed some time to think as I walked slowly down Fourth Avenue towards Flinders Parade. It had been a very big day. There was a lot to take in. One thing I remember is making a promise to myself that I would never forget our daughter's birthday: the 10th of November 1970. I must never, ever forget this day, I must etch this in my mind, so I started saying a mantra: 10th, 11th, 70; 10th, 11th, 70. Never ever forget that day. You must *never* forget it.

9 | WHAT COMES NEXT?

My parents never knew that I'd visited Boothville Hospital that night and I was never going to tell them either. Some days later my mother nonchalantly asked, "So what's happening with Fran having the baby then?" In reality she would have been contacted by Fran's mother and told of the birth, so she probably knew full well 'what was happening'.

I replied, "I have no idea." And that was all I had to say as I was pretty much emotionally shut down. Mum knew Fran had had our child, I think she just wanted to know what was actually happening with that child and was making sure we (she) weren't going to be burdened by it. I believe she wanted to be sure our child was being given away *as arranged*. I think, considering all the emotions surrounding birth, my mother would have been worried that something may have changed, or 'someone' may have said, "Keep your baby and we'll work it out." That would have been too much for Mother to handle. It was a fine line everyone was walking.

Mum, being her stoic self, reiterated her long held stance and said, "Well, now that's over you can get on with your life and forget all about it. You'll get over it in time." Full stop, fucking full stop!! Surely not, surely this is not how life works? If it was, at seventeen years of age, I was severely disappointed in it already. And so, we are all just meant to pretend this didn't happen and move on, right?

I thought, *What the fuck?* How could you possibly be so cruel? You are talking about a little life, my daughter, part of my being, your granddaughter in fact, your own flesh and blood. How insensitive!

I couldn't help but think that if my parents had seen our baby when she was a brand-new arrival, wrapped up in her little crib, they couldn't have possibly let her be given away. Mind you, I am assuming the best in human nature here which I've found, through bitter experience, does not add up to much sometimes. Confronting that would have been a turning point for them, but it never happened because what is left unseen does not have to be dealt with emotionally. So, they were good citizens, and the system designed to have us separated worked to perfection for them. Meanwhile Fran's heart and my heart broke.

If I hadn't already done it, I was certainly hardening my heart and resolve towards my parents now, my child's grandparents, no less. Why didn't they care? The questions never stopped, and for me the feeling of being alone and abandoned was huge. Apart from having Fran in my life, I was now a loner. I no longer needed anyone else, I certainly didn't trust anyone anymore, especially anyone connected to a church, and I knew I had to rely

9 | WHAT COMES NEXT?

on myself—and my wits—from here on out. From this point on, life for Fran and me would never be the same. It was a defining moment.

Over the preceding few days Fran's four older sisters had visited her at Boothville. They all would have seen our baby, and as far as I am aware, they too were happy for her to be adopted as no one ever said otherwise. More toeing the mutual decision lines that were already in place. More of the blinkered view of, *'This is what's in place, so we won't question it in any way'*. Bloody sheep, baa!

A visit from Fran's sister, Jan, provided another twist of fate and brought more skeletons out of the closet. It turned out that Jan had also given birth at Boothville Hospital some ten years previously and had given her son up for adoption through the same system. Who knew? No one knew. It was a another cover up which came out because of the birth of our child. Another secret hidden from the world. And something which would provide us with another 'problem' that would test us much later down the track.

During this visit Jan commented to Fran that she should get shot of me and that I was no good. I held this against her for years, until she developed cancer later in life and we softened towards each other. She reckons I gave her the best hugs when she was near the end of her life and battling that debilitating disease.

I still couldn't help but think if, and that's a very BIG if, someone had stood up to support us what a different story this could have been. We could have brought our child up; it would have been hard at first, but I'm as sure as the day is long that we would have had a lovely life together. We were both young, but not unintelligent, I was also working in a trade and earning a solid, if not lean, wage. I had a defined career path, Fran had previously worked as a dental assistant, the possibilities could have been endless, but not one person stood up to support us. The disappointment I felt towards these people was profound. It still is.

Elsewhere in a Brisbane city office a fee is paid for our child in the form of an *Adoption Order Section 7, form 10 under the Queensland Adoption of Children Acts 1964 to 1967*. There is a number at the top right corner that reads **29748**, that's how our child is identified.

In the coming days there were to be two birth certificates issued, one pre-adoption and one post-adoption, where the adoptive parents could change the baby's name to whatever suited them. It was a given that the child would be renamed using their surname. It was apparently optional to retain the child's first name. Our child, named by Fran as Priscilla Anderson, was to be renamed by her new parents: first name, middle name, and last name. There was, therefore, no trace of Fran and me to be found except on the pre-adoption birth certificate which would be secreted away in a filing cabinet in a city building along with thousands, if not tens of thousands, of others. As mentioned in the

9 | WHAT COMES NEXT?

previous chapter, as the father of our child, I did not rate a mention on any of those documents. But who cared? Nobody cared ...

Fran returned home eight days after the birth to her mother's house in Nashville. She would get a job shortly afterward working at a specialised dental practice in Queen Street in the city centre, prior to it becoming a shopping mall. And I carried on working in my apprenticeship. We were still kept apart.

On the morning of Monday, the 23rd of November 1970 our daughter's new parents would receive a notice via the mail that there was a child ready for them to pick up at the Boothville Salvation Army Hospital in Windsor. The child, a girl, had been born some thirteen days earlier and was in excellent health, and she had a wisp of blonde hair and brown eyes—according to the Department of Adoptions paperwork I was granted access to many years later.

This would be the culmination of a two-year wait, and she would be the second adopted child who would take up residence with their family on an island off the coast of Brisbane. Their first child was a son who had been adopted some three years earlier in 1967, because they were unable to have children. The Department of Childrens' Services had been working hard to ensure there was some resemblance between the two adopted children as the boy also had blonde hair and brown eyes.

The Post Adoption Birth Certificate would contain her

new name, and she was a most welcome addition to the family. As a baby she had severe colic, a similar condition to heartburn, which would cause her some upset, and according to her big brother she cried the house down through it all on an all too regular basis. One has to wonder if her new environment, new surrounds, and new smells had something to do with her being upset, let alone being separated from her birth mother. It had to have had an effect, but the fact remains, our child was a gift from us to them.

Human connection. What does that mean to you? Even at the tender age of sixteen years I knew for certain we humans are meant to be connected, we are intrinsically meant to be with others who are like us. In fact, we crave it, we look for it in all things. My family brought me up with these values, but then they threw them out with the dishwater when the narrative didn't suit them.

I was undoubtably and unashamedly connected to my daughter from the day I found out she existed. I fully expected human nature to kick in and show kindness and empathy to me at the news that Fran and I were going to have a child. The reverse of that happened. I was basically unplugged from human connection by our parents, and the pastor of the church, and the Salvation Army, and the nurses and the matrons, and our relatives and our friends. Every single one of these people were responsible for kicking me (us) in the guts and leaving

9 | What Comes Next?

me (us) to fend for ourselves.

At sixteen years of age, I was astounded by this revelation, and still am, that humans could be so cruel especially concerning a new life, one of their own species. It seemed to me then, as now, that I was disconnected from human connection, a vital system that sustains us. And I've never been plugged back in.

The other interesting thing about this is that I loved my daughter with all my heart from the point of her conception. We finally met when she turned twenty-one, and I had loved her for all those twenty-one years. I guess I expected her to love me as soon as we met in the same way, but she didn't and that's not her fault. More disconnection.

Thirty-six years later I'm still waiting to be plugged into a real and meaningful relationship with her in a father and daughter way. That may never happen. So, it remains that I felt a loss of connection at sixteen and it continues to the present day, fifty-five years later. I find that very sad indeed. Is it my fault? Should I have gotten over this by now? It's a question that keeps me wondering twenty-four hours a day, seven days a week, 365 days a year, year in and year out. It's a question that may never be answered.

10 | A 'Clean Break'

The adoption process in the 70's was based around secrecy and what was seen as a 'Clean Break'. The prevailing ideology was that the best outcome for both the child and the birth parents was a complete separation with the adoptive parents raising the child as if they were their own biological child. There was an emphasis on finding suitable adoptive parents, often married couples with secure incomes, who could provide a stable and loving home.

The *Adoption of Children Amendment Act* came into operation on 1st May 1970 ensuring that the Child Welfare Department must approve of the adoptive parents before an adoption order could be granted, and recognise that the mother of an illegitimate child should have sole consent to the adoption, and not the putative father.

All of this is very fine and splendid on a surface level, but it does not take into account the fact that a mother and child have bonded over the nine-month period of gestation.

There are many doctors and psychologists who agree that bonding begins before birth, and there is both a psychological and physiological—not to mention a spiritual—connection at play here. The relationship between a natural birth mother and her child is both conscious and permanent.

> 'The resultant separation at birth from the natural mother results in experience of abandonment and loss in the unconscious minds of these children. The child **does** experience being left by its biological mother and being handed over to what you would term strangers. The child will experience this separation as trauma and rejection and therefore manifest in feelings of emotional and behavioural problems and of loss. These feelings can be conscious or unconscious, but they are deep seated, no less.'
> (Excerpt from *The Primal Wound* by Nancy Newton Verrier)

I'm sure that our daughter's new parents followed due process when applying to adopt a child, as they had done previously with their son, and qualified with flying colours on every level. BUT they would definitely not have been counselled as to what the future may bring for that child being separated from her natural parents. It just wasn't within the system to do that back then. So how would they deal with the questions in the future? Only time would tell.

According to the Australian Institute of Health and Welfare nearly 10,000 babies were adopted in Australia in 1970, an increase of forty-five percent over the four preceding years. Many of these adoptions were forced adoptions, as is the case with our child.

The excerpt below from the 'Forced Adoptions in Australia' fact sheet puts the numbers into greater perspective.

> 'While separation by adoption continues, approximately 150,000 adoptions occurred during the peak period of 1951 - 1975 (although forced adoption is not limited to this period).'
> *https://www.dss.gov.au/system/files/resources/fact-sheet-history-and-experiences-forced-adoption.pdf*

By way of comparison there were only 201 adoptions in Australia in the year 2023.

Here's some information based on research undertaken by the Australian Institute of Family Studies (AIFS) about the effects of forced adoption and forced family separation:

> While adoption practices in Australia have undergone considerable change since the 1970s, the effects of forced adoption and forced family separation are still very much a part of the lives of the many thousands of people involved. The impacts of forced adoption and family separation are diverse and long-lasting, not only for mothers and fathers separated from a child by adoption, but also for the adult sons and daughters who were adopted as babies, and their extended family members. The most common effects of forced

adoption are deeply psychological and emotional, and include:

- depression;
- anxiety-related conditions;
- complex or pathological grief and loss;
- post-traumatic stress disorder (PTSD; including complex PTSD);
- abandonment, identity and attachment disorders; and
- personality disorders (Kenny et al., 2012).

Accordingly, the needs of people affected by forced adoptions are diverse and ongoing, ranging from obtaining records or purely information-seeking activities by involved parties, to highly complex trauma-related issues requiring long-term support. Further, these effects can present themselves at varying stages and levels of severity throughout an individual's adoption journey.

It is essential that those affected be supported by well trained and integrated mental health services and other specialist services.

Source: https://aifs.gov.au/research/research-reports/forced-adoption-national-practice-principles

During Julia Gillard's term as Prime Minister of Australia,

10 | A 'Clean Break'

her government was lobbied through a parliamentary and senate enquiry to make a National Apology for Forced Adoptions on the 21st of March 2013 at the Great Hall of Parliament House, Canberra. Queensland Premier Campbell Newman also made an apology in Parliament on the 27th of November 2012. These apologies mean nothing to me personally. It was just waffle from a bureaucrat in a suit. How could they possibly know what it feels like?

Late in 2024 I applied for the birth information for my daughter, out of interest apart from anything else. I received this information three months later in January 2025 from the Department of Families, Disability Services and Child Safety. Parts of the documentation were hand written sheets logging our baby's progress, feeding habits, problems, and even recording when she was hungry. The notable thing here is that she was showing positive signs in all areas on most days and ticking all the right boxes. However, in the days after Fran left Boothville problems started to arise—the notes say, "Unsettled following feed at 9:00 a.m.," and "Is not contented and fusses at a.m. feeds and very difficult to burp."

I would find it hard to be convinced that a baby would not be affected by the following:

- ❖ The fact that there was no form of bonding allowed with her birth mother in her first week

- ❖ That she was bottle-fed on formula—not on her mother's milk as nature intended

- ❖ The fact that she was left in the care of nurses and others (the inmates) when Fran vacated the premises

- ❖ The impact on our child when she was handed over to her adoptive parents: the new smells, a new environment, a new routine to settle into

In no way am I casting aspersions upon the folk who adopted our child. However, reading the documents detailing our baby's first week of life was incredibly sad for me; it affected me physically and mentally. There was a heaviness hanging over me in that moment. I couldn't concentrate properly or set myself tasks, which was really unusual for me because I'm usually highly motivated. The effects were—are—real.

Our daughter was kept at Boothville for thirteen days until the 23rd of November 1970, when she was discharged for adoption.

Who were these adoptive parents? Where did they live? How old were they? Why couldn't they have children of their own? So many questions. Deep, deep questions no one had an answer for, but the major one hanging on our lips was, if we gave her up now was there any chance we could get her back? Was there any way she could be fostered out and we could get her back later?

We were hanging on by a thread, scratching at ideas,

10 | A 'CLEAN BREAK'

desperation hung in the air as we searched for an answer ... but there was no resolution forthcoming. Our baby's fate had already been sealed by others, it was way, way out of our control. It would appear I had no rights as the child's father; no one ever asked me to sign for her adoption. What were MY rights? Did I have any? Was this because I was still considered a minor—underage at sixteen?

As we were to discover twenty years later, I had every right to have seen my daughter back then, and they could not have refused me. We learned that we could have rescinded the adoption order within thirty days and regained custody of our child (according to the Department of Childrens' Services) if we'd had the knowledge or the resources to do so.

The information I received from the Department of Families, Disability Services and Child Safety included the Adoption Order and Adoption Transfer Form which included registering the adoptive parents details, dates, etc. There was also a form giving me permission to rightfully apply for our child's pre-adoption birth certificate through the Department of Births, Deaths and Marriages. I applied for this also.

Within the documentation it stated that Fran signed the adoption papers on the 16th of November 1970 and also that—

> 1. *I understand that the nature and effect of such order will be to deprive me permanently of my*

parental rights in relation to the said child.

2. *No other person is required to consent to the adoption of the said child.* [No one ever asked me if I'd like to be party to this contract—it was like I did not exist.]

There is an additional section which would have required my consent as the child's father, but that area was crossed out, deleted—in other words *not* required.

None of the papers I received (rightfully applying as the birth father) included my name as the father of our child, as apparently was the system in the 1970s. To discover this fact after wondering about it for all these years was humiliating and soul destroying to say the least. But I'm hardly surprised by this—it's actually what I expected, even so it doesn't lessen the gravitas. I applied for the paperwork because I could, I **am** my child's father, regardless, and I identified myself as such to gain access to the documents. That paperwork clearly states, "Thank you for your application for adoption information about **your** daughter ..."

So, the wash up is that in 1970 I was not acknowledged, or required in any way, as our child's birth father. I had no part in the whole process. I had no say. But now in 2025 I am fully recognised, and the paper trail confirms that they did know who I was. Very strange how things have changed, for the better I might add.

A further note on the documentation: the Adoption Order form affirms our daughter's name as Priscilla

10 | A 'CLEAN BREAK'

Anderson. Another form states her birth name change from Priscilla Anderson to her adopted name, and who her adoptive parents were. But there is no such person as Priscilla Anderson, she does not exist anymore. The only place she continues to reside is in the hearts and minds of her birth parents.

She assumed her new identity just thirteen days after she was born on the 10th of November 1970. She left Boothville Salvation Army Hospital as yet another statistic of the forced adoption era and was adopted into a new family and a new life to become another person.

In my discussions over the years with my daughter she has never recognised her former name as Priscilla Anderson. It's a subject we have never broached. She may not know about the information I discovered, or be aware it's available to her; it's a route she's never been down. She is who she is now, and that's the end of the story. I don't personally need her to accept her name at birth, but I believe that not knowing it is a denial of who she actually is. I believe she is masking that part of her own past.

A couple of the adult adoptees I've met through Jigsaw Queensland Inc. Post Adoption Centre, have taken steps to have their birth father's name registered and their birth certificate amended through Births, Deaths and Marriages. I think this is a beautiful and touching step to take, fully acknowledging them as part of their history and life. I don't know that I'd go down that road myself, I don't think I could broach the subject with my daughter, and I'm not sure how she'd react to that. She considered her adoptive father as her dad, not me. And there I go beating myself up over it again.

The Pre-Adoption Birth certificate I applied for gave me another jolt back to reality. I was looking forward to receiving it, hopeful my name would be on it. Hope can be a cruel master, as upon opening the mail the section where 'Father of child' is listed it is totally blank. Nothing, no one entered. I gave it a few days to settle in then rang the Department of Adoptions, who were lovely to deal with. The woman I spoke with confirmed that—as was the case with the information I had received earlier—I was not required to be part of the Adoption Order, therefore, my name was not entered on the paperwork. That was the system in 1970 and that was that. She looked further into my files and paperwork and confirmed to me that my full name Philip John Kenward was in fact recorded (but not registered) at the time of birth as the Father. Another surprise, they knew of me, but I was ignored, and my name was suppressed.

The other stand-out fact on the Pre-Adoption Birth Certificate was Fran's age, stated as eighteen years old. Nothing else was stated, such as occupation, which would normally appear on a 'standard' birth certificate.

The Age of Consent in 1970 in Queensland was sixteen. This originates from the *Queensland Criminal Code Act 1899*. Fran and I had both consented. The age of

10 | A 'Clean Break'

adulthood was considered (by society) to be at twenty-one years of age and was usually celebrated as such by Australian families.

At the time of our baby's birth Fran was eighteen years and three months old, she would have been legally entitled to keep our child, but she was coerced and forced to place her for adoption against her (our) will. After all, this is called 'The Era of Forced Adoptions' for a reason. She was, however, considered old enough to hold down a job, get a driver's licence, and get married.

In January 1993 my friend and running partner, Ivan, confirmed to me that the old Baptist Church system was alive and well when he was greeted with the news that his seventeen-year-old daughter was 'in trouble'. With his family being members of the local Baptist Church, he would see the age-old, well worn-out scenarios and solutions brought out of the cupboard and put into place. She was instructed that she would be leaving home and that the child would be adopted. Even in the '90s, the system within the church had held onto these archaic ideals. It would seem that not much had changed.

Fran and I decided we could not stand by and watch this happen without saying something, and though Ivan did not know we had been reunited with our daughter, we decided an approach to his daughter in private was appropriate. We conveyed our story down to the last detail, including how we had recently been reunited with our adopted daughter, and of the pain and anguish we had endured for more than twenty years at the hands of someone else making decisions on our behalf. It would seem our chat had no influence on her decision, as some six months later she adopted out her child. What a sad indictment on the system, and a decision we were sure she would regret in time.

11 | THE AFTERMATH

There was an eerie silence descending over what had happened to us over the past twelve months, and it was deafening. No one mentioned what had happened to us, to either of us. It was just as though it hadn't happened. What pregnancy? What birth? Trauma, what trauma? Everyone around us, including family and friends, seemed happy *not* to discuss any of it. It was all swept under the carpet, things were quiet, very quiet. My mother would reiterate the standard line to me of, "Just forget it, you'll get over it." Really? So, I should just grin and bear it, hey? I would definitely not take that on board. How could one ever forget such a momentous event?

It would seem we had to get on with our lives and that's just what we did. I kept on living at home, working at the factory on day shift and going to TAFE college at night. Fran returned home to live with her mother in Nashville. Separated lives, still. Other people were still so much in control of what we did, and it was as frustrating as hell. Did our parents think we'd just drift apart? How would that be possible? Did they not think we were connected by having a relationship which brought our beautiful child into being? Mind boggling!!

At around Christmas time 1970, I was seventeen and some significant events took place. Firstly, I got my first car, a Morris Minor 850. I bought it from a guy I worked with for the princely sum of forty dollars, and although I didn't possess a driver's licence or a learner's permit I still got to drive it regularly on the road with Dad seated beside me. It suited me actually because I was going against the system and it felt good.

My relationship with Dad was tentative to say the very least, we were at arm's length now, we both knew it and it was strained. Dad letting me get the car didn't come with any reassurance, but it may have been his way of trying to breach the divide between us. He never said as much. We always had the bonnet up, fiddling with this and that, changing the oil, checking the spark plugs and stuff. Other than that, it got driven every afternoon after work up and down the side of our house and around the backyard of the Fourth Avenue property. It was excellent practice for me although I'm not sure the neighbours would agree, up and down that driveway, backward and forward endlessly.

The second event took place shortly after the Kenward family had sat down to Christmas lunch and would highlight just how much tension and frustration the events of the past year had taken on my father, a usually even-tempered man.

The meal our family of five had just finished had been the usual traditional English-style Christmas roast lunch

11 | THE AFTERMATH

that included a large turkey with all the trimmings. Hot Christmas pudding and custard followed, the thrupenny bits found inside the pudding too. I guess we were all trying to normalise what had gone before. No matter how hot the Australian summers were, and they could be stinking hot, we always sat through this ritual feast regardless and enjoyed it. It must have been something to do with being British.

When it came time to do the washing up afterwards, I was asked to dry the dishes while one of my younger sisters washed up. Christine and I always made the washing up a bit of fun, lathering each other with the dishwashing bubbles as we worked, good fun and a great laugh.

No problem, I thought, as I left the dining room to retrieve a couple of fresh tea towels from the linen closet with a spring in my step and feeling sated from the huge meal. Unfortunately, our linen closet was outside of the main back door of the house annexed into a new modern toilet and bathroom extension which had recently been completed. This had seen the demise of the outdoor toilet facilities, the Thunderbox down the backyard was no more.

Without giving it a second thought, the back door I'd left ajar behind me slammed shut, caught by a gust of wind. Within what seemed like a split second my normally placid Father burst through the door and had me bailed up forcibly by the throat against the wall, and with an angry inflection in his voice was threatening to throw me down the stairs if anything like that ever happened again. It was a guttural response; I'd never seen such rage from Dad especially since it was an innocent mistake on my part. He told me gruffly to get on with the job I'd been given. No amount of explaining would remedy this, although it was enough to highlight to me how close we were living to the edge, on tenterhooks in fact.

Everything was quiet in the house after this, we resumed our duties in the kitchen as I was told to, but I was quite shaken, it just added to my new level of frailty. All the events that had taken place of late served to keep me on edge with my nerves jangled, that feeling of anxiousness rising within me and at times taking me over. Home didn't feel like a safe space anymore. I seriously wanted to run like hell, but I didn't know how or where to, I felt constrained somehow.

Fran and I had stayed in contact by writing letters to one another for the last few months. Fran's mother, Emily, knew we had remained in touch so one day asked through a letter from Fran if I'd like to visit at the house in Nashville. This was very open ended and not a resumption of our relationship by any means. It was a test, not a surety.

Weeks passed challenging my patience, but then a date and time was set, so I tentatively approached the house in Darling Street on a sunny Saturday afternoon and

11 | The Aftermath

stepped up and knocked on the glass-paned front door. I had a feeling of queasy apprehension of what would come next and what sort of reception I'd receive. In my position it all felt slightly precarious, and I wasn't really sure which way this might go. Emily opened the door, but didn't open it far enough to let me in, it was just barely ajar and definitely not welcoming. Looking at me directly through the narrows, and with much consternation in her eyes, the high stakes game started. Were we playing chess or Russian roulette? Either way it felt very intense. The first question directed at me with imperious authority was, "What are your intentions for my daughter, Philip?"

The suggestion she'd just made had such an obvious answer but, of course, she wouldn't have known that we'd always maintained contact, albeit deceptively behind her back. I felt a slight inkling of guilt over this, but Emily held checkmate.

Emily obviously knew she had the power to veto us seeing each other, so for me it was a 'tread very carefully' scenario. Her question had caught me on the hop, but I answered succinctly that I loved Fran and hoped we'd be able to see each other again, and that I'd be happy to marry her daughter when the time was right, soon if possible. Emily gingerly stepped back on her heels to let me in through the door, she didn't open it wide, I had to squeeze between her and the door itself as politely as possible. I'd entered the room to a stony disquiet with a bitterness still hanging in the air.

Emily soon retreated to the next room whilst I stood there like a lamppost pondering our tacit agreement, waiting to see Fran who was holed up around the corner in the kitchen. Emily was looking back quizzically over her shoulder as she left the room wondering if she was doing the right thing, I knew it, she knew it, not only for us but for herself also. Maybe in her eyes I'd already upset the balance once and she hoped the decision she'd just made would not lead to yet more regret.

Emily never mentioned anything about her daughter's pregnancy or the birth or the adoption which had all happened within the last few tumultuous weeks. Her lips were sealed, and were likely to stay that way to all and sundry. It's just what she did and what she was comfortable with. I did wonder at the time if she ever thought about our baby, her grandchild, no less.

We gladly resumed our relationship that day even though we both realised immediately that a huge part of each of us was missing. Fran's tummy, so expanded from pregnancy with our child, was no more; she looked thin and worn down by the toll she'd paid. We'd had a lot of time apart over the past few months and talked endlessly about how we would never forget our child, the topic always never far from our lips. We wondered how she was getting along, where she was, was she happy, what was she looking like now, and where was she living?

The loss of our child was still palpable, we felt it in every

11 | THE AFTERMATH

inch of our beings, and I'd have to say we weren't convinced our baby was having the better life that she was promised, it just wasn't sitting right. She should have been with us, her rightful parents no matter how young we were. Even in the aftermath we asked each other, time and again, had we done the right thing? Guilt was slowly creeping into us, and it pervaded our everyday life. Was there anything we could have done differently? Why were ALL these people against us? Even though we had the solid bond of our love between us, we were both drowning in a sea of emotion and there was nothing we could do about it. Looking back now I would not be surprised if we both suffered a degree of Post Traumatic Stress Disorder (PTSD).

So many questions and so much catching up to do. No matter how destabilising the past year had been, our connection to one another had never diminished and we closed ranks firmly to the outside world. The grief we both wore may not have shown itself because everyone had told us *just to get on with it*. But the scars were on the inside where no one could see them. Little did anyone realise it, but those scars would NEVER heal.

Fast-forward a couple of years to 1972. I was eighteen now, and in my third year of my Fitting and Turning apprenticeship; Fran was nineteen and back working as an assistant for a specialist in the dental profession in Brisbane city. We were both earning the princely sum of about thirty dollars each per week. I'd recently bought my first motorcycle, a brand-new Honda XL100 (small capacity), and was riding it unlicensed. I used to pick Fran up from work most afternoons and drop her down the street from where she lived. Mum Anderson definitely would not have approved of such behaviour! I used to double Fran everywhere on the thing. We even did trips up the coast and into the hinterland on it. One Sunday we ventured out, two-up, to Lakeside International Raceway at Kurwongbah to watch the motorcycle road races, the place was packed with every kind of bike, and I loved the whole scene.

The trip home though was a different story; the police blockaded the road out and were pulling every motorcycle over for a licence check. Panic! I didn't *actually* have a bike licence—learner's permit yes, licence no—and I was doubling. Shite. Suddenly, I noticed a lot of women in bike gear walking past ... odd. I asked a biker near me what was going on, he said there must be a lot of guys riding unlicensed. Great.

The bikers creed then kicked in, people were starting to sidle up to others who did have a licence to help each other out. One bad motherfucker of a bikie said he'd vouch for me while Fran joined the exodus of pillion riders. Yes, officer, we are riding together. There was a collective sigh of relief as we took off, no tickets written to pick up our moles ... oops sorry, I mean partners.

Our daughter was now two years old and the time since

11 | The Aftermath

her birth had flown by.

At this time, I was attending TAFE college two to three nights a week from 6 p.m. to 9 p.m., but I was actually enjoying the process. Such a change from the boredom of school days, and the funny thing is that I was starting to excel at subjects I'd never previously had any interest in, like mathematical equations, formulas, and the like. I finally began to understand how these formerly mysterious entities could be used and applied in real engineering situations.

Besides that, one of my teachers, Mr Nicholes, a wily old fox, took a shine to me because I was showing a flair for understanding engineering drawings. He had a way of engaging with students, the likes of which I'd never come across before in my school years. His method was simple: "You lot get through the work at hand, then we'll spend half an hour talking about how to hot cars up (through applying engineering principals)." Then he'd let us go early too. What a guy! He taught my younger brother, Trevor, in the following years and Mr Nicholes shared fond memories of me, his 'A' class student.

This newly-found interest also got me into the drawing office at my workplace to study drafting, and my flair for it would see me stay in the office much longer than any other apprentice in the place. Finally, I had found my forte and a way to direct my energy and my arty side. I was also away from the noise and filth of the workshop floor. Naturally, all of the other apprentices on the factory floor envied me.

Another area I was directing my energy into was local karate classes, of the style called Shukokai. I absolutely loved martial arts, and over a period of time I was graded up to a blue belt—one before brown. I loved the discipline of it and the camaraderie of this ancient art form. It was keeping me as fit as a fiddle two or three nights a week and was providing an outlet for at least some of the animosity I'd felt through our ordeals. It provided a way to channel and release the torment of all my inner demons, so it was good to let go of the aggression at least in a positive direction. Having achieved a ranking of blue belt, I subsequently took on teaching duties of younger students, which I enjoyed.

1972 would see the Apollo 16 space mission leave Cape Canaveral and head to the moon, the first of The Godfather movies on the big screen, and Don McLean releasing the song, *American Pie*.

It was also the year that would see Fran and I married. My work colleagues presented me with a gift, and added in an accompanying speech that I was doing things the 'wrong' way around. Usually apprentices finished their traineeship first, then got married. I was in my third year so I had another two years to go, but I couldn't have cared less what they thought.

The wedding was a pretty small affair held in Gordon Park, on Brisbane's northside, and it was presided over by Pastor Maxwell Howard whom we had known from

11 | The Aftermath

our early years at Sandgate Baptist Church. Family and a few close friends were invited. It was hardly lavish, and it was catered for by the women folk of the church.

Me and Fran at our wedding in 1972

We took off on our honeymoon to Caloundra in my trusty grey 1961 lowered FB Holden sedan, which had matt black stripes hand painted down the bonnet. They were a bit wobbly, but it wasn't a bad attempt. The car had been converted to a floor gear-shift, the only problem with that was the gear linkages kept on falling off through vibration, which meant the gear shift lever would come off in my hand at the most inopportune moments. I'd then have to stick my fingers through the hole in the floor to actually change gear. Tricky, one hand on the wheel, leaning to the left, still keeping an eye on the road ahead, foot on the clutch which made threatening sounds of gears engaging as I attempted to change gears with my fingers. Snick it up a gear then retrieve my hand which would now be all greasy.

We rented a run-down old house in the back streets and stayed for a week. It was nowhere near the beach, couldn't even see it, but we were young and had plenty of energy, so it didn't matter how far away the beach was. We'd amble along holding hands and feeling very much together in our new locale. We both loved the feeling of being married, it was so nice to be connected and to show the world that we were meant to be together, despite everyone's efforts to keep us apart. We had to endure cold showers for the first few days though due to our naivety and because we couldn't figure out where the power switch was for the hot water system! A previous tenant had turned it off, so to get around this we boiled water in saucepans on the stove and had hot, albeit shallow baths—very inventive.

From about the time I was eighteen years old the Vietnam War had been raging for about ten years; it was always in the headlines. Battles were being fought over territory, and the biggest conflicts for Australian troops were in Long Tan, La Drang and Saigon. It was a war that was never going to be won by anyone, no matter how much money and manpower was thrown at it. The real enemy were the Viet Cong, and they were always going to outsmart United States and Australian army personnel in an unfamiliar landscape.

They say that the Viet Cong could smell the aftershave on the American soldiers a country mile away, so they may have been easy pray for ambushes in a jungle setting. Half of them were probably jacked up on drugs

11 | The Aftermath

too. Young men, it wasn't their war, but like me they probably felt duty bound, doing it for their country's pride. A lot of good it did them with the soldiers of all colours and creeds hardly getting paid any recognition for the job they did when they got back home. The Vietnam war was also a divisive subject in Australia, and a lot of serving soldiers suffered after returning home.

Nevertheless, I still wanted to join up, I saw it as my duty to go and defend our country. My dad had fought in World War II as a British Army recruit from the United Kingdom—good 'Old Blighty'. His service would see him leave his home town and family in Bexhill-on-Sea in Sussex to do his initial training in Ireland, and then serve as a truck driver and an ambulance driver on the battle fields of Palestine in the Middle East. I thought the honourable thing to do was to follow in his footsteps. Heaven knows the scenes he must have witnessed during his time there. Needless to say, he would never talk about it.

Australia's involvement in the Vietnam War lasted from 1962 to 1973. 60,000 Australian troops were deployed there, 521 died and 3000 were injured.
[Source: National Archives of Australia]

During this time the Australian government had a draft system in place whereby I could have been called up, but the end of the National Service Scheme in 1972, and the end of Australia's involvement in the war in 1973, put paid to that.

It was also a time of great social and political change, such as the sacking of Labor Prime Minister Gough Whitlam by Sir Jim Kerr, the Governor General, in cahoots with Malcom Fraser, the Leader of the Liberal Opposition in November 1975.

I was actually quite disappointed that I couldn't enlist—I mistakenly saw only the glory of war and just wanted to go and kill the enemy, whoever they may have been! Hindsight would say it was probably a good thing that I didn't go, as I'm pretty sure I would have come back severely traumatised had I seen any real action. Or just be dead. In the years after the war, I came across a lot of guys who had been to Vietnam and had seen live action—they were pretty fucked up.

As for Fran and me, we were established in a strong relationship, and we had each other's back. We knew it and so did anyone else who might challenge it. We'd put the walls up around us as a self-preservation measure and no one was let in; we were cast iron tight. It was now 1975 and our daughter would have been just about to start school. Almost as soon as I finished my apprenticeship we decided to travel to New Zealand for work. We were told that New Zealand was suffering from a shortage of 'skilled machinists' so I applied to an advert in the Brisbane Courier Mail newspaper. After a short interview with an agency in the city, we found ourselves packing to go on our first adventure overseas in a few short weeks' time.

11 | The Aftermath

It was an electrifying time and things were moving quickly; we had to sell the car, pack up everything and put other goods into storage. We packed limited 'stuff' to take with us and sent it off in boxes by ship. We excitedly paid for our own airfares with Air New Zealand, hopeful of being reimbursed. At the time there was a reciprocal arrangement for travellers between Australia and New Zealand, as no passports were required to travel either way. Fabulous.

There was another incident that drove us to leave Australia. We used to ride with a couple of friends all the time, they were two brothers who were both married, and we all had motorcycles. We all got along famously ... until one of the wives approached us to join them in wife-swapping parties! We said a definite NO to this, and we felt betrayed by them, and thus ended the friendship. Another reason to leave, you see. How 'seventies'!

We both knew the reality of it though, we were running away from the experience of losing our child and how we perceived that people around us—who we'd thought we could trust—had treated us. I wanted to get as far away from them as possible. Distance seemed like a logical solution.

12 | Travel Bugs

Although the idea sounded good at first, the job in New Zealand didn't really work out. I'd come from the clean, tidy, and quiet environment of a drawing office, but found myself working in the back of a dirty machine shop on a large lathe machining cast iron housings. I had absolutely loved the flight over the Tasman Sea to New Zealand, I thought it was the bee's knees being a first-time traveller. Everything was new and exciting. But by contrast, this was the filthiest job I'd ever had, and I wasn't happy. So much for being a 'skilled machinist'.

Long hours, dirty, dirty work, the machines screaming around me, a stranger in a new town, we knew no one. It turns out that they couldn't find anyone locally to actually stay at this job for longer than a few weeks, so I was 'imported' from Australia under the guise of paying our return airfares (a few hundred dollars at the time) at the end of my tenure—if we stayed for the twelve-month contract. The agent had found us a unit to rent, which we paid the bond and rent for. I didn't stay long, maybe three weeks, and quit the job much to the displeasure of the agent concerned, and we forfeited our promised refund of airfares.

Although this was a bit of a shock it didn't unnerve either of us, we were surprisingly calm about it and felt quietly optimistic. I think we both felt empowered by our joint decision as we were calling the shots now and not just bowing to pressure from others.

We could have run back home to Australia with our tails between our legs, but we didn't, and we decided to stick with the plan and bravely make a go of it in the 'Land of the Long White Cloud'. Besides this, we had also imported my near new Honda 360 motorcycle to New Zealand, so we had immediate transport on arrival. I had packaged the bike up and had it flown it into Auckland airport, which was relatively cheap and simply done. I got a roadworthy certificate and registered the bike within a couple of days. I had researched prior to leaving Brisbane that motorcycle prices in New Zealand at the time were a lot higher than in Australia, so even if I sold the bike, I probably wouldn't have lost anything on the sale. I really didn't want to have to package the thing up again and spend more money sending it back to Brisbane.

In the scheme of things, it wasn't really a big deal as a couple of weeks later we'd both landed new jobs. I found a job working in a drawing office for Burns and Ferral, a large stainless steel fabrication shop in Penrose in Auckland, and Fran was working at a dry cleaners in Greenlane. We moved into a one-bedroom flat on the Great South Road in Greenlane and basically had nothing much other than the clothes we stood up in, but we set up our own little nest and got on with OUR lives with no one to answer to or influence us. It was fun and a little taste of freedom, which let us totally be ourselves for once and find our own way. The brand-new radio cassette player we'd treated ourselves to and bought duty free at the airport was always in the background tuned to Radio Hauraki, a popular pirate FM radio station.

We had no friends and certainly no one around us to judge us, and that suited us both just fine. Wow, what a change. Milk was four cents a pint and was deliciously creamy; New Zealand ice cream from the dairy (the Kiwi term for corner shop) was cheap too. These two items, combined with the colder climate, would see both of us pile on the weight for a time, or maybe we were just plain contented ... for once. Due to the poor weather—or was that unpredictable weather—we decided to buy a car to get around in if/when the weather was inclement, which was most of the time. Our weapon of choice was a 1950's split-windscreen, very old, light blue and white VW Kombi van we named, 'Herbie's Mother'. So now we could tour the country sightseeing the wonders of the North Island, albeit at a slow pace due to the underpowered engine, but at least in relative comfort.

One of the more notable events happened in our second year in Auckland at the Western Springs arena, which usually hosted speedway events. Neil Diamond came to the small islands of New Zealand for a series of gigs, and we were there to see him live that night in the open air, our first real concert. His double album, *Hot August Night*, had been released in 1972, which he played live at the Greek Theatre in Los Angeles, so most of his material came from that, now very famous, album. We sat on a grass hill with a group of work friends and the music just blew me away. His music and lyrics reached in and grabbed my heart and pulled it so hard that I couldn't believe the emotional effect it was having on me. I found the whole thing overwhelming and had tears running down my cheeks with nearly every song. The concert was far from a downer, but rather it lifted my spirits far higher than any other phenomenon I'd experienced to date. It was the start of my musical journey as a release from everything.

Two years later, in 1977, and having made many new friends, we toured both North and South islands and had lots of new adventures. I had raced a Yamaha RD250 motorcycle in modified production at the Pukekohe Park Raceway south of Auckland, entered the New Lynn road racing Ceramco Grand Prix around blocked off streets, and drag raced at the Meremere Dragway drag racing track in the Bombay Hills. We also got to see the Marlboro Series road racing in both Auckland and Christchurch where overseas stars figured on a packed programme—Pat Hennen and a fifteen-year-old Randy Mamola from the US included. We saw the great Mike Hailwood test a Yamaha TZ750 at Ruapuna Raceway prior to him going to the Isle of Man TT (Tourist Trophy) the following year, which was exactly where I was

12 | Travel Bugs

planning to be.

Leaving New Zealand didn't come easy as we'd settled into a new life all of our own making there, but we had a wider plan to travel further afield so we returned to Brisbane for a couple of months.

In Brisbane I was working on night shift for the extra cash machining railway wheels in a workshop in Geebung, and doing some drawing work, while Fran was working part-time in a bakery. The plan was to be heading to England to travel more. I was born there so I had history to follow up on, and relatives to visit.

My biggest aim, first and foremost, was to get to England to see my favourite international motorcycle road racing personalities and visit the Isle of Man TT. Famous names of road racing heroes I'd only previously read about in motorcycle magazines like Mike Hailwood, Barry Sheene, Phil Read, and Giacomo Agostini to name but a few. There was no television coverage of these races available back then.

I could have stayed in England forever, it felt familiar and felt like home. It also felt like a safe haven away from the hurt back in Australia. The time we stayed there seemed short and flew by, but I actually fitted in there and belonged, life was good. Of course we did all the touristy things like visiting castles, cathedrals, etc., and travelling to all corners of England, Scotland, Wales and Ireland. 1978 was also big for music in England and the world scene, it was a time when bands like The Cars,

Van Halen, The Police and Dire Straits released their first albums.

Me and Fran in England, 1978

I did get to live my dreams with two trips to the Isle of Man to watch the Isle of Man TT in 1978 and 1979. Dad had come over to the UK for a holiday too, so we arranged to go to the TT races together. The future saw me return to motorcycling nirvana in 2009, and in 2011 for the 100th Anniversary of the first event.

Mike 'The Bike' Hailwood, who was a nine-times GP winning legend, returned to road racing after a layoff of eleven years, and won the TT on a Sports Motorcycles Ducati 900 NCR—which had been purpose-built for that race—and a Suzuki RG500 in different classes. I also attended the Transatlantic Trophy races at Brands Hatch and Mallory Park and saw the greats in the USA vs England races. Kenny Roberts, Steve Baker, Dave

12 | Travel Bugs

Aldana, and Johnny Cecotto, to name but a few. I also went to Europe to watch two rounds of the 500cc World Championship, one at the famous TT Circuit Assen in Holland, and the other at Circuit de Spa-Francorchamps in Belgium. I was a great fan of Barry Sheene, the Brit.

Two trips around Europe followed. We had many plans of touring in camper vans, and bought and sold a couple of likely vehicles: two VW Kombi's (Herbie's Other Mothers) and a Bedford van. In the end we decided, with time running out, to sell the vans and do guided coach trips to squeeze in as much of Europe as we could before returning home to Brisbane. Because of our limited budget we decided to fly home on Laker Airways via Los Angeles. We spent three weeks in America touring California in a rented Toyota Corolla, with a side trip down into Tijuana, Mexico. The trip back home included stopping off in New Zealand to catch up with friends for a few days too. It was Christmas 1979—we arrived with two dollars left in our pockets, dead broke, but what a time we'd had.

I had to return to Australia because my visa had run out and there was no option other than returning to Australian soil to renew it. At the time I held a British passport with only a three-year time limit to be out of the country, otherwise I wouldn't be allowed back in without immigrating (again) which would have proven difficult.

Having spent two-and-a-half years in England by this time, the plan was to come back to Australia, get my paperwork sorted, and go back to England as soon as humanly possible and tour as much of the world as we could again. The travel bug had bitten deep. England was by now familiar, seemed to have plenty of work and provided a good base and jump-off spot to get to most places in Europe. There was so much we hadn't seen yet and what we had seen and experienced had just whetted our appetite to see more of it. Such a big wide world AND we both knew deep down we were still running from our past. That shadow hung over us still and was pretty motivating to just keep moving. Our daughter was now ten years old, and we wondered often what her life was like.

Back in Brisbane in January 1980 and we had both quickly landed jobs to start stashing money away. We'd planned maybe a three-month stint before we'd be leaving again.

Little did I know our plans would change very quickly with the announcement that Fran was pregnant. Our focus changed completely. We got caught up in the process of building a house on the piece of land we'd previously brought in Petrie, north of Brisbane, which originally cost $7,500 in 1973. Even though we had no money, as in zero savings, and we were just working for wages, the Queensland Housing Commission provided us a loan of around $25,000 for the build at 17 percent interest. It had helped our cause that we had collateral in the block of land. We moved into that brand new home one week before the twins were born with the bare

12 | Travel Bugs

minimum setup of second-hand furniture.

The babies, twin daughters, arrived late in October 1980 and were a gift. I had always taken it, rightly or wrongly, that we'd been given these two children because we'd lost our first child. The universe can work in strange ways. It was also conspiring in a way one would not have thought possible, but then if you look at the theory of 'six degrees of separation', maybe anything is conceivable.

My sister's boyfriend, Paul, was studying to become a primary school teacher, part of which entailed him doing his teacher training on an island just off the coast of Brisbane. It was 1982 and he was assigned to the primary school, the only school on the island. One of the children at the school, in Paul's class, was our very own daughter. He didn't know it, she didn't know it, but there was a connection no less. Our daughter was in that class; what were the chances? Paul was twenty-four years old, and she was twelve years old. My, how fate works. Paul and my sister married soon after and both went on to be teachers, and many years later a photo would surface of Paul standing in the schoolyard surrounded by the children. Standing at the front proudly, if not quietly, was our daughter. How small is the world?

Around this time our daughter realised she was adopted. She found out one day after school when other kids, her friends, had mentioned that this might be the case. She asked her parents straight, and they confirmed she was, in fact, adopted. They didn't try to cover it up and were open and honest about it. Our daughter received this news joyfully and didn't question it any further. She actually considered herself lucky to have two sets of parents. This might have brought up questions in her young mind, such as: Why was I given away? Why did my other parents not want me? Her feelings of loss and abandonment may have manifested from this point, even at a subconscious level. The sense of separation from her birth parents from her time of birth could not logically be denied now. This revelation must have raised more questions than answers for her.

By contrast, and through psychological studies, it has been shown that adoptees often feel as though they don't belong in their adopted families, this family of strangers, especially where there are no physical similarities. They often feel they are not understood and that they don't fit in. Was this the case for my daughter? Or did she just carry on blissfully unaware and happy? What her adoptive parents told our daughter about the reasons behind her adoption is not known. Did they mention that her biological mother was unable to look after her? This will probably remain a mystery, but it could have affected her later in life.

Established in our own home and having a family of our own was blissful, if not hard work, having twins. It was pretty demanding and after a full day at work I'd get both the babies handed to me as Fran was worn out. I'd lay back with a baby over each shoulder in our one and only

12 | Travel Bugs

reclining-but-very-second-hand seat to quieten them down. Five years later a son would be born into our family too, but by this time I had graduated to a wicker rocking chair. All plans to return overseas were thwarted, but that was okay as we were happy and settled into family life.

Fast-forward to 1991, a pretty standard family-centric life. I was working as a Design Draftsman at ACF and Shirleys Fertilizers in Pinkenba, while Fran looked after the kid's full time.

We had applied to the Department of Childrens' Services for information relating to our daughter's adoption in 1970. We informed them that we were together and married hoping this might elevate our case. We received a standard form letter stating the date our daughter was adopted and that she was living in an island community offshore from Brisbane. It would not have been hard to work out which island that would have been. Moreton Island had approximately 180 residents in the 90s, while Stradbroke Island had a community of approximately 2000 residents, a sand mining operation, schools, and a tourist industry supporting it. All the information we received was non-identifying, so it didn't really tell us much. We didn't give it too much more thought, nor would we search any further or deeper as the last thing we wanted to do was upset the balance of a newly established nuclear family. We'd just have to wait a little longer.

13 | Adoption Laws

1991—We heard on the ABC news that the adoption laws were to be changed in Queensland. This change would allow contact between adopted persons and their biological parents. This was to give us some glimmer of hope and reignite our chances of finding our daughter, who was now twenty-one years old. So, we applied for contact and left it at that, but we were not very optimistic or even hopeful about the outcome. We were also members of Jigsaw Queensland, a support group in Brisbane dedicated to finding and reuniting adopted persons and families. They had some levels of success in reuniting adopted persons with their birth families, and it was heartwarming to read about these matches and reunions in their monthly newsletters.

Thinking nothing more of it, and not knowing what the chances might be, we continued on with our lives until one afternoon the phone rang. I picked up, a lady named Marie from the Department of Childrens' Services was at the other end, she introduced herself and then announced she'd found our daughter, and we had a match. Not believing my ears I scrambled to find Fran to get her on the line and hear the news for herself.

To say that we were both in a state of shock would be an

understatement. Our daughter, our long-lost child was out there somewhere, and she wanted to meet us. This was surreal, unbelievable. I just wanted to dance and shout and scream, such was the shock and joy of it all that overcame us both.

Within a few weeks a date was set for us to have an interview at the Department of Childrens' Services offices in the city to see if a meeting between us and our daughter was possible. At this point in the process, it was definitely not a foregone conclusion that everything would fall into place. We didn't get our hopes up too high or get too excited, but we hung on to the thoughts that everything would be okay, maybe ... and we'd do what was required of us to make it come to fruition. We also did not tell a soul this momentous news; we kept it to ourselves. It was too good a piece of news to share or have to explain to others.

The day of our interview. We were told our daughter would be attending her interview on the same day, but earlier. We had both dressed to impress and I remember as we walked down Edward Street in Brisbane toward the offices looking at everyone who passed us intently thinking, *'that could be her, or that could be her'*. We had no idea at the time what our daughter looked like, and we were clutching at straws. Our excitement level, though, was off the dial and our nerves a little rattled.

The big old building, possibly turn of the century, had great sandstone columns to the exterior, dirtied by years

13 | Adoption Laws

of passing city traffic. The interior of the building appeared to be old and in dire need of a facelift, as many similar aged buildings in Brisbane did. The most outstanding feature though was a long row of very high but narrow casement-style timber windows placed evenly, which were letting in great shafts of sunlight into the dull and musty interior. These huge portals of glass led up to ultra-high ceilings, which were in turn decorated with lavish, patterned, polished timber architraves.

We met Marie, our assigned officer, on the third floor and proceeded to a small office. Marie was lovely and said she'd interviewed our daughter earlier that day. Her adoptive parents had also agreed for the meet up.

As a part of the interview procedure, and I guess for the department officer to be sure that we wanted to go through this for all the 'right' reasons, we were requested to explain our past. We dug deep and dragged up every detail right from the beginning. It wasn't hard, we remembered everything in fine detail. All the 'whys and wherefores', who said what, who and what influenced the decision to give our child up in what was typically a forced adoption.

We both got quite emotional and were a little surprised by that, I guess all the feelings we were now talking about openly and freely had been bottled up for over twenty years. This was virtually the first time we'd both sat down to explain our past to someone who wasn't sitting in judgement or even expressing their opinion on the matter, but someone who was going to reconnect the past for us and, we thought, right all the wrongs against us.

There were also some curly questions added to Marie's repertoire. When she asked us point blank, "What would happen if you met your daughter and didn't like her?" It caught us a little off guard. We answered without even having to think first, that we had never considered that a possibility. There were some major revelations, such as that when our baby was born I had every right to see my child, and in fact no one could have legally stopped me. She added that we could have rescinded the Adoption Order within thirty days of the birth date. Pity no one told us about these things at the time, we quipped. Marie also took it upon herself to point out that our daughter's boyfriend had attended an earlier interview and seemed a tad over-protective; we weren't quite sure what to make of this fact.

She commented that our daughter was a beautiful young woman with a lovely nature. She was also looking forward to meeting us, her natural parents, and was surprised to get the news that we were actually together. We left a package of photos for her. We were also given her home phone number and were apparently free to call her. This just seemed too good to be true, could this really be happening, real contact? A date was set for a reunion in a few weeks' time on Anzac Day 1991.

13 | Adoption Laws

Later that day I received another phone call at work from the department to say our daughter had brought photos in and I could pick them up. She had obviously picked ours up too. I opened the envelope as soon as I got out of the building and was amazed as I leafed through them how much our daughter looked like me. I was quite shocked—it was like looking at my younger self. I was also happy to see that in every photo our daughter was smiling; she looked happy and content.

That night we rang our daughter's home phone. It took a great deal of courage to do that as we had no idea what the protocol was with this. We started out nervously but eased into a conversation mostly centred around our preceding meetings with the department. It was so lovely to talk to our daughter on the end of a telephone. Who knew it could have ever come around? We were still pinching ourselves that this was really happening, it seemed so surreal. We both ended the conversation saying it was nice to talk.

The following weekend Fran and I and our kids visited my parents' house in Sandgate. It was customary, even though the house was expansive, that most serious talking got done around the table in the small kitchen near the rear entry of the house. There was one very serious conversation about to take place. I started out by announcing nervously to my mum and my dad, "I've got something very important to tell you … [pause] … you know the child we gave up way back when we were young? Well, we've found her …" That statement hung in the air; it just stopped all time.

The look of shock and horror on their faces was incalculable. They were lost for words, so I continued and explained about the government changing the laws for access to adoptees and that we'd been contacted by the Department of Childrens' Services. We let them know we'd soon be meeting up with our daughter in the next few weeks and reminded them that she was now twenty-one years old.

Still no comment from my parents who looked aghast. My parents didn't know what to say or what to do. They didn't know how to handle the bombshell I'd just delivered right into their unsuspecting laps.

Not much else was said, there wasn't much else to say other than the fact that they might have to face some of their old demons. I knew I had lit a fire by bringing up the past, but equally I did not want to hurt my parents. They'd have to deal with the news between themselves. Also, I didn't bring the photos we had received; at this point they were private and classified for our eyes only. I guess I didn't want to invite comment on who she was and what she looked like, that would have been all too much.

On another visit a few weeks later we entered the same kitchen with the kids. This time though Dad immediately said, "Can you come downstairs for a moment? There's something I need to show you." I obliged thinking he'd show me the latest tool he bought for his workshop or

13 | Adoption Laws

maybe something in his veggie patch.

At the bottom of the stairs and standing next to his beloved greenhouse he reached out, looked me straight in the eyes and said, "I'm so sorry about what happened with your baby all those years ago." He had tears welling in his eyes and a wavering of emotion in his voice; it was the most heartfelt apology I had ever witnessed in my life. It could have possibly been the only apology I'd ever received. We had a huge hug. I would have liked to have cried in his arms, but I didn't. I know I probably should have, given the circumstances, but for some reason the tears just weren't there. Maybe the past had caught me up, all that pain, all those memories had hardened me, and I knew it. I didn't like it, but that's where I was at.

For my dad, he had obviously been thinking a lot about the announcement I'd made a few weeks earlier and had processed it in his own way. I think he wanted to deal with it as such, man to man, father to son, something he'd not confronted prior to that day. My father apologising to me in the backyard at Flinders Parade—it was heartfelt and honest and raw. That simple gesture healed a thousand wrongs between us and our relationship improved ten-fold from that day onwards. I was just a teenager when it all happened to me, so I respected Dad for his words and for being so contrite. I found the love from my dad that was lost so long ago.

Mum well, she never apologised, never has. For her, being part of, or an instigator in, us having to give up our child twenty-one years previously was done and dusted and to be forgotten, brushed under the carpet and such. It still rang in my ears, "You'll get over it, just get on with your life." As stoic and set in her ways as she is, I'm not sure I can forgive her for this. She'll take it to her grave not knowing a thing about how all of this has affected me. She has NO idea of the reasons I'm a little obtuse or indifferent.

Fran's mother, Emily, was also living in Sandgate at this time and was becoming a little frail as she approached her eighties. People can be cruel. In her later years Fran's mother had a few problems, as we humans tend to do, in dealing with this thing called *life*; it was nothing out of the ordinary, just a few things she couldn't get her head around. She suffered fits of depression, and who wouldn't after the life she had lived and the hardships she had endured. She had, after all, raised five children—all girls—almost single-handedly and had to deal with a violet alcoholic husband at the same time.

Along the way 'someone', whether it be family member or a doctor, had decided it was in her best interest to start a course of electric shock treatment. How anyone could think this type of treatment was going to be a quick fix is quite beyond me. I'd be the first to admit after the therapy that, when she was good, she was really good, but conversely when she was down, the downs were worse than they ever were before. You could see the struggles she endured trying to dig herself out of the hole she'd found herself in. We are partly to blame for this;

13 | ADOPTION LAWS

we all should have taken better care of her.

We volunteered to take her for a drive one Sunday afternoon and whilst travelling brought up the same subject of the search for our daughter and how we'd found her through the changes to the state government laws. She took this in quietly and contemplatively, but said nothing. One would hazard a guess that, as with my parents, she was also taken back a little. It would have been a lot of information to process on the spot and an unlikely subject for her to have to deal with immediately.

The afternoon was pleasant enough if not a little quiet. Upon returning to her boarding home, we followed her up the ramp walking slowly. Midway up she turned to face us and said to us both that giving our baby up was one of her biggest regrets in life. Wow, that statement could have blown us away with a feather!! A small gesture but a heartfelt one, no less, and it mended our relationship with her somewhat from that point onwards. Fran's mother would never get the chance to meet her granddaughter in the flesh as she passed away before it was possible.

It's funny too, that the apologies we had received from my dad and Fran's mum had healed our relationships with them almost immediately, a bit like someone had waved a magic wand over us and undone a lot of hurt. For me, Fran's mother, Emily, and I got on really well after our initial—what would you say—falling out. She thought I was really funny and loved a laugh. She also admired me that I had hung around and had not just left Fran in the lurch after our baby was born.

For me, it no longer actually mattered what anyone, including our parents, said or didn't say, the damage had already been done over twenty years ago. The clock couldn't be turned back. They were the ones who were going to have to face the very real fact that their granddaughter was alive and well and about to appear before their eyes in the coming weeks. How they would deal with that was obviously up to them. Did they have demons? Would they feel any shame and guilt? They must have some emotions about it, but how would they deal with it when they were confronted with the actual person they had affected? I didn't really care, the ball was in their court, and I certainly had enough of my own feelings to deal with.

What's more, and it's something we gave little credence to at the time, how would our daughter react to them, her real grandparents, once she knew the truth? And, by God, she was going to hear the truth direct from me! The questions were starting to pile up and we hadn't even met her yet.

14 | THE RESURRECTION

This part of the story started in 1967 when I was around fourteen years old, and hasn't ended yet!

My dad had big plans for us when I was young, as I was the eldest of five children. Dad worked shift work, sometimes sixteen hours a day doing double shifts. Subsequently I didn't see much of him as he often worked night shifts to earn more money.

When I did see Dad, it was fleeting and mostly on weekends. When he was home, he always had a project on around the house, be it working on maintaining the house or in the garden. Dad worked physically hard, and I can remember him spreading truckloads of ashes throughout the yard to build up the ground level to protect our property from inundation by sea water, as we were only some two-hundred metres from the sea front.

He also took it upon himself to restump our high-set home in Fourth Avenue in Sandgate. This was a merciless task, first to prop the house up directly underneath, remove the rotted timber stumps and replace them with huge concrete stumps to support the house. The new concrete stumps had to have very deep footings dug out which would naturally fill up with sea water because the water table was very high there. The stumps, which probably weighed in excess of sixty kilograms, would then be manoeuvred into place using a special trolley made up of old car tyres and wheels and a steel plate slide. Once propped up, the stump would then be concreted in place. Dad also mixed the concrete by hand in a wheelbarrow. I tried to help where I could.

I became a 'people pleaser' very early in my life. Dad would be working on various projects around the house or garden and would often ask me to run an errand to pick up some nails or screws of various sizes from the local hardware shop. I'd take off like a bat out of hell running barefoot to the shops, money safely tucked in my pockets, buy the parts and run back just as fast. Part of the reason I ran was because the footpath or bitumen on the road surface was so hot under my bare feet that it seemed far more efficient to glide over its surface.

All I ever wanted to do was to please my dad, but when I arrived back he'd say, "Why do you run everywhere?" I just wanted him to acknowledge me and that I'd done something good, I guess. But that didn't happen, and I think he saw me as a useless bugger being that I was at that sort of goofy age. He even called me 'Useless Doosless' on one occasion after I made a hack of helping him paint the back stairs. Seemed a bit like water off a duck's back at the time and it didn't overly worry me. I knew Dad was a real perfectionist and everything had to be done his way and the right way. I guess I was still learning, there was a lot to learn.

14 | The Resurrection

With all the overtime Dad worked and the projects he had on it's a wonder he had any time at all for his family of five children.

One weekend though, Dad asked if I'd like to go to the Brisbane Car Show at the Exhibition Grounds near the city. I wasn't much interested in cars, but we gravitated to the racing car section and got talking to a group of enthusiasts on the Formula Minor car club display. This really piqued Dad's interest as the open-wheeler cars were powered by motorcycle engines from British bikes: Norton and Triumph twins, Velocette KTT's, Matchless G50 singles, and the like. The engines were run on methanol fuel and 'suped up' to give them much more performance and horsepower than standard. We ended up joining the car club. I remember Dad asking me succinctly on the trip home if I'd like to be a racing driver The answer was a solid YES from me.

We started going to the Mount Cotton Hillclimb and Lakeside International Raceway on family outings. I loved the smell, the sound, the excitement, and the drivers, every one of them a character. It opened up a whole new world to me. Initially we would start the build on one car. The club had peaked so much public interest through the car show that they started building standard chassis frames for members to purchase. Dad bought a chassis which came complete with suspension arms and a roll bar. The plan was for us to have a racing car each, down the track. What a thrill that would have been, both of us on track, but unfortunately it was never to come to fruition.

In 1968, when I was fifteen years old, we started work on *Chassis Number One*, we had an engine out of a Matchless motorcycle—around the 1955 vintage—to install in it, and some brake and suspension parts from an old Triumph Herald. The club committee was very helpful to new and aspiring members and would make home visits to help in the build and suggest how and where to source parts. The cars were cobbled together using many different makes of car parts that were available.

A year later, *Chassis Number Two*, known as 'The Tardis' after the time machine from Doctor Who, was purchased. This would be a quicker build and would get us both on track much sooner ... or so we thought. The Tardis was bought as a complete rolling racing car without an engine as the owner was building a new car, he kept his Velocette 500c engine for that.

One Saturday morning Dad took me along to a 'speed shop' in Windsor to buy me a racing helmet. It was a white open-face Bell American helmet, and probably cost Dad a small fortune back then. It had a peak, like the professionals wore, and a leather and silk padded interior. I can still remember the smell of it. It was the perfect fit and had the precise look for an aspiring racing driver.

1970 would prove to be a turning point in all of our lives when Fran announced her pregnancy to the world. All

14 | The Resurrection

work would stop immediately on the racing car projects, the dream stalled. It became a sore point between Dad and I and the cars were covered over with dust sheets, maybe to never see daylight again. I knew deep down that I had disappointed my dad, and we never broached the subject of the cars from that point onwards. After the birth of our child and her subsequent adoption, Fran and I went overseas for nearly four-and-a-half years as the cars sat idle gathering dust under Dad's house, never to be touched by him.

This is one story that does have a silver lining though as the racing car project was restarted in 1998, some thirty years after its inception. By this time, I was well established in my job as a draftsman, living in a house I had designed and we'd built in Albany Creek, and had three teenaged children. I was rifling around under Dad's house one day looking for some tools and uncovered the Tardis which was tucked away in a corner. It brought my memories as a teenager flooding back. I respectfully asked Dad if we should rebuild the car, and he enthusiastically agreed we should.

The car was initially taken to our house in Albany Creek to be completely dismantled down to a bare chassis. Dad, and my brother Trevor, would come over on weekends and work on the many components, rebuilding brake parts, welding mounting brackets, tuning the suspension, etc., and installing the

Matchless engine which had sat idle for all that time.

Dad, at the wheel of the racing car

Around twelve months later the car was ready for its first outing. We took it to a Lakeside International Raceway practice day in Kurwongbah and I did a few laps in it as a shakedown run and to see if any problems arose. None did, so we all patted ourselves on the back for a job well done. It also looked, sounded, and smelt a treat especially running methanol racing fuel through its open exhaust. The car was then driven in competition at the Mount Cotton Hillclimb in 1999 by me, with Dad watching intently. Trevor also drove the car and Dad was as pleased as punch to watch both his sons' achievements. The dream became reality that day.

The car was driven regularly in a historic open-wheel class at Mount Cotton Hillclimb for two years. It set reasonable lap times in the '60+ Second Bracket' category comparable to when it had previously run, until it was again shelved, this time due to the cost of rebuilding old gear. Being an older car and using fifty-year-old parts, it used to break components like rear

14 | The Resurrection

axles on a monotonous basis. It was getting more expensive to fix every time. So, then the car was resigned to idle sit in Dad's garage for another eighteen years, propped up on stands.

Other projects were to take priority though, as Dad also owned a 1954 Matchless motorcycle which was in about a thousand parts in his shed. The 'Three Brothers', as we coined ourselves—Dad, Trevor, and me—started a two-year ground-up rebuild of the old bike. Dad also copped the nickname 'Mr Tap Tap' during this rebuild since he was always tapping away at something in the shed. I was dubbed 'Mr Tap Tap Junior'; I didn't mind wearing that mantle.

The bike looked resplendent in its new deep black paint with gold pinstripes on the bodywork. The newly chromed parts glistened in the sun. It was standing on fresh Dunlop TT100 tyres and was ready to roll.

It was 'happy days' the week we got the bike started and running. We had to take the bike to a vintage bike club member's house to tweak the bike's ignition and retighten the odd loose bolts—typical Dad. It took three hefty kicks to get the bike to fire, and the look on Dad's eighty-year-old face seeing that bike running was so very memorable. The bike sat in the driveway ticking over beautifully, so it was nice to see all the work we'd done finally come to fruition.

Dad passed away a week later from a heart attack. The Matchless now resides in the National Motorcycle

Museum in Nabiac, NSW, on display. It has a plaque describing the build and showing a photo of us with the bike we'd all built.

Fast-forward to 2018 and I was contacted by the MG Car club to see if we could display the racing car at the 50th anniversary of the Hillclimb, and they said they didn't mind if the car was running or not.

 As part of Dad's legacy, I wanted to resurrect the racing car for the second time and actually run it at the hill. I had a determination like never before to run the car, mostly to honour Dad. This would mean all hands on deck as we only had a few months to get her up and running. My two girls loved being involved and helped with sanding down and painting the old girl to make her look good. Interestingly, my brother Trevor struggled more than any of us with working in Dad's shed; this was due to everything in that garage being in the same place that Dad had left it prior to his passing. All his tools were still there: his files, hammers and drills. It felt like someone had just snatched Dad away and left a void.

Me with the pit crew

14 | The Resurrection

The car was filled with methanol fuel, the oil levels were checked, and then with a gentle push from my Pit Crew—my twin daughters—it fired up on the driveway the weekend before the meeting and everything worked as it should have. The car was ready for an outing. It was put in a Bunnings hire trailer for the trip, and amazingly it fitted into the dual-wheeled trailer perfectly.

The meeting was run at Mount Cotton in February 2018. Part of the history of the car was displayed with the car in a static display. The original car, built by Murray Caterer from Toowoomba, ran in 1968; later it was owned and driven by Chris Lake and his family for many years before we purchased the car. The Tardis had run at the first meeting fifty years ago and here it was ready to attack the hill again.

I had two runs at the Hillclimb along with an array of beautiful vintage and historic racing cars. Was it worth the effort? Oh yes, definitely! The first run was pretty gentle so as not to stress the car (I have what's known as 'mechanical sympathy') and for me to get used to the track again. I also found out heading down the very steep decline of the second hill heading into the tight right-handed hairpin bend that the brakes we'd only partially looked at didn't actually work very well at all. The car basically had no brakes, so I relied on the gearbox and engine braking to slow the pace somewhat. All drivers were told to take it easy as this was just a fun, easy day.

On the second run I decided to go for it and drive the car

like it was meant to be driven in competition years before. As I made my way around the circuit on my own in that cockpit, cresting the peaks and descending the hills at full throttle, I thought back and hoped I'd made my dad proud. His son had realised his dreams and really was a racing driver.

Returning to the pits after our sixty seconds of fame we found the car had shaken off the air filter pod on the carburettor due to excessive vibration. It was also sitting in an ever-increasing puddle of oil leaking out of the engine. We thought it was pretty typical that a fitting would come loose like that because Dad was known for not tightening bolts up correctly. If he was watching us, he would have had the last laugh.

Two things had come out of all of this, not only had we rebuilt a racing car, and a vintage motorcycle, together but we had rebuilt our relationship as a father and son(s) during those times in the garage. We had resurrected the racing car, the dream, and the relationship. I know Dad would have been proud. The dream never died, it had just been put on hold.

15 | MEETING UP

All is not what it seems, or what you may have dreamt of.

We met on Anzac Day, the 25th of April 1991 in the Botanic Gardens in Brisbane city. Over twenty years had passed since our daughter's birth and yet here we were ready to meet her. The weeks prior were a flurry of emotions and sleepless nights. Would she like us (me)? Would she just want to meet up and then have nothing to do with us again? Oh God, I hoped not. Did she hold it against us for giving her up?

There's those age-old emotions showing their ugly heads again, the guilt and the shame. God, how I wished they would leave me alone. Would we get along? How would she take the news of having real brothers and sisters? Did she need to know any medical history? Did she have any medical issues that may have been familial? How was her life growing up? What was her childhood like? Her parents? What was she doing now? Where was she living ? Oh boy, so many questions and we were scrambling for answers. We were definitely overthinking this.

The fact that it was Anzac Day didn't help as many streets had been blocked to host commemoration parades in Brisbane's CBD. Off-street parking was now a nightmare, and our meetup time was of the essence, and there was no way I was going to be late for this. We found a carpark in the streets near to the gardens and left the car. I remember thinking as we walked quickly away from it that I couldn't have cared less if the car, an old Holden Kingswood wagon, (not the Kingswood!) was there or not when I came back, such was the intensity of the emotions running on the day. We'd just deal with that later and maybe have to retrieve the car from a towing company's holding yard. The cost wouldn't have mattered; it was inconsequential to the enormity of what else was happening.

We walked with some pace to the gates near the river end of the gardens for our 10 a.m. rendezvous. The yachts moored along the Brisbane River set a picture-perfect scene as a backdrop. Traffic rushed, as always, across the Story Bridge in the distance as the river glistened below it. It was a beautiful fine Brisbane day, if not a little steamy.

We approached the large iron-clad main gates at the central entrance to the gardens on Alice Street and waited. We were half an hour early, that was good. We had time to take in the freshly turned over garden beds nearby ready to be planted out with new flowers, I loved the smell of fresh soil. As there had only been a few weeks between our interview at the Department of Childrens' Services and today we hadn't overly studied the photos we'd received, so we were guessing what she

15 | Meeting Up

might look like now in the flesh. All we knew was a time and a place to meet up. We then saw a young person walking towards us, she was early too but there was no mistaking her. Her look, her walk, the way she carried herself, unmistakably one in a million. She introduced herself and we did likewise as Phil and Fran. Even that seemed too weird to contemplate. We were astute enough to *not* be saying, "Hi, I'm your dad and this is your mum!"

A concept that I strongly subscribe to, and many police forces around the world use, is a system called 'Racial profiling and psychological outcomes'. As humans, we have this innately set up in our own personalities or our DNA, and it gives us the ability to know within five seconds of meeting someone, by subtle indicators, if they are good or bad. This was VERY good, it was so easy to tell.

As we met, Fran embraced her saying, "Hello." I did the same very happily, it was a big, beautiful, meaningful hug full of emotion and connectedness. I didn't want to let go, I wanted this hug to last forever and I was so glad it was a hug and not a handshake, as that may have set a different tone. We stood and chatted but soon adjourned to a bench under one of the massive poinciana trees nearby. The reality is that we all had shaking legs and we actually needed to sit down. There was so much to say, ask, enquire, and it probably came out as total mush. We discussed the process we'd all been through to get to this point over the past few weeks through the Department of Childrens' Services and how lovely the staff had been. We were all totally amazed to have had a match, our daughter more so since she'd only been registered for one-and-a-half-weeks before she received the news that we were registered and willing to meet. We all seemed genuinely pleased to have met one another, I think there was fascination for each of us. She seemed as interested in us, in our faces, in our gesticulations and movements, as we were in hers. It was uncanny and there was absolutely no doubt whatsoever she was our offspring.

Sometime into our conversation the subject came up as to what we had originally named her. We told her that at Boothville Hospital Fran had named her Priscilla and that we had both agreed on this name when she was born. This came as a shock as she thought her birth certificate had her registered as Victoria! I think all three of us were taken aback by this, but it could have been a proving point as to the goings on at Boothville by the Salvation Army staff: manipulating records so people would not be found at a later date. At this point in time, I had not applied for birth records or for our daughter's pre-adoption birth certificate so we were none the wiser either.

We told her outright that we didn't ever imagine finding her, and yet here we stood together some twenty years later. Our daughter also told us that she had always intended on finding her birth parents, even from the very first time she had been informed by her parents that she

15 | Meeting Up

was adopted. She didn't see this as a negative and thought how lucky she had been to have two sets of parents. If there was ever a time to be moved to tears then this was it and I guess we were looking for positive affirmations as well. She had such an upbeat attitude in every way as far as we could tell. In the short time we had come to know her, as we sat on that park bench, we started to feel very close to her. There seemed to be no distance between us at this precise moment in time, but nevertheless the huge gap which separated us did remain intact, and I think we were all aware of it encroaching upon us.

Whether what she had said about being lucky with her adoption was reality or not was yet to be tested. At the time I really wanted to believe what our daughter was telling us, even though my own self-doubt was telling me otherwise. Was she just saying that to allay our fears? I knew I was a definite 'people pleaser' (see more about this in Chapter 20, *Mental Incidentals*) so would it be possible that this trait was also ingrained into her, deep in her DNA, in fact? Through my own experience I thought it inconceivable that our child was totally unaffected by being adopted, but time would tell.

On a personal note, every time I looked into her eyes, I could not help but feel a tinge of guilt and a pain deep in my heart, a sensation the likes of which I had never experienced before. I questioned myself again and again, how could we have possibly given her up as a baby? This most beautiful young woman who had grown from those beginnings. I also felt a strong sense of anger rise up, directed at those who had used coercion against us in the past. If only they could see us now.

I had a package to present to her on the day too, it was something I had bought the day she turned eighteen, around three years earlier, and I thought now might be the appropriate time to give her the gift as a memento of the day. She opened it tentatively, and was surprised to find a necklace with a silver '18' pendant that had a diamond as the centrepiece. For me it was an indication to say we hadn't forgotten her and we remembered all of her birthdays, every single last one of them. She looked a little more than shocked by the gift, I was unsure if she was taken aback by its value in dollar terms or the meaning I had placed on it. What exactly she was thinking would remain a mystery, but there was an air of defensiveness hanging in the air now. Little would my daughter have realised, but I would have given up *everything*, all my worldly possessions, all my travels and experiences, to have her back in my life. Nothing else mattered more than her to me right now—she just didn't know it.

An interesting point here is that having raised my other three children, even though they were still young at this stage, as a parent you get a pretty good handle on their train of thoughts. You learn the way they process things, having been together from day one. In other words, you can just about gauge what your offspring are actually thinking. So, this reaction was something I didn't quite

15 | Meeting Up

know how to deal with. I didn't expect a gushing, loving thank you, but I wasn't prepared for the reaction I did get. It was one of the first signs that a gap of twenty-one years apart was telling indeed. This was another poignant reminder in the adoption process that you lose your child as a baby and then meet them as an adult.

The conversation turned to her adoptive parents, her brothers and sisters, where she grew up on the island in a wonderful seaside community, and what her life had been like growing up there. We were drinking every detail in at this point. I thought about how lovely her parents must be as human beings, not only to have raised her, but also to have supported her in every way in her quest to find her natural parents.

During the conversation, which by now had been going on for about two hours, we noticed a young guy constantly riding past us on a pushbike, carefully watching us, looking our way as he passed by slowly. What was all this about? Turns out he was our daughter's boyfriend so we called him over. He was obviously keeping an eye on proceedings and looking after her best interests. Is it possible we could have been that scary or intimidating? I think by this point in my life I was a pretty good judge of character so I'd have to say he seemed a little too overprotective, and this had also been indicated by the officer at the department a week prior. She had said to watch him ... a thought-provoking statement! It was interesting, to say the least, to add someone else into the mix now, and I wasn't sure

I liked it. He was definitely defensive and came across a bit macho, it changed the vibe of our meeting. I was as wary of him as he was of us. Two alpha-males circling one another working out who has the power, no doubt. Our time with our girl was basically cut short by this incursion. But, as with all things, we had to accept the circumstances as they were; once again we were powerless and we didn't control the running of this narrative. All we really had in this situation was to be open and honest. Many years later at a Jigsaw open meeting we were to find out that adoptees often use other people close to them as 'human shields'. I had no idea of this fact at the time of our meeting, there was a lot I didn't know, obviously. She may not have been aware of this either, perhaps she did it subconsciously for her own self-protection or well-being.

The boyfriend was probably blissfully unaware that he was being thrust into the role of our daughter's protector, or shield, and being young he may not have been emotionally equipped to deal with the situation at hand. The reality of it is, who would be?! He was just there doing what humans do, I guess: showing his bravado, playing his part, protecting our daughter from the monsters that we could have been. It made the situation difficult and a different experience to what we'd expected. Feelings were already on edge and this only added another element to the tension.

We decided to adjourn for lunch to the café inside the garden complex and talked some more covering every

15 | Meeting Up

subject imaginable. We then told her she had twin sisters and a brother. To say she was somewhat surprised would be an understatement, but we asked if she'd like to meet them, and if today would be appropriate. No pressure and there was definitely no rush. It turned out she was happy to meet our other kids, so we arrived at our home in Petrie with both in tow.

Our three kids—my ten-year-old twin girls and five-year-old son—were being looked after that day by my younger sister, Elaine, so they all greeted her with open arms and this was just beautiful to watch as our siblings reunited too. There was no doubt at all they were brothers and sisters; it stuck out by a country mile. The visit was short as they had to drive home to the other side of Brisbane.

What a lovely day it had been, we left each other as we had met: with an expressive hug and hopes that we'd see one another again soon. We stood on the footpath to wave our goodbyes. What a day, what an absolute rollercoaster of a day! Emotions had run high, so much ground was covered in a few short hours, but above all else we'd met our child who we'd thought lost to us.

Life with children has a funny way of bringing everything back into perspective and grounding you as a parent. There were now our other three kids who commanded our full attention. With dinner sorted, bathtime done and bedtime stories read, it was time for us to reflect on this momentous day. We went through every scenario replaying the day, delighting in every minute and what it brought us. We both agreed that she was the most charming person with exquisite manners, so lovely. Her other parents must be so proud of her and we thought they had done a beautiful job bringing her up.

Something was bugging me though, something deep inside was gnawing away at my guts and I felt uneasy, if not a little more than anxious. Something I realised I hadn't said to my daughter during the day was eating me alive and I felt I just had to get it out. The fatalist in me, the voice in my head saying, *You might die tomorrow,* said it needed to be dealt with now, now as in today, right away. The upshot was a phone call at around 8 p.m. I spoke to her female flatmate first who was obviously screening calls, but she quickly put her on the line.

Our daughter was a bit quizzical about why I'd be ringing, there was a tone I detected which said, *Haven't we just spent the day together, what now?!* So, getting this vibe, I deliberately made sure it was a short conversation, we went through the niceties of the day, so lovely to meet you etc., but I ended up just blurting it out and said, "That before this day had ended, I just had to say *I love you.*" … Silence … a long silence. She then quickly replied, "That's nice," … more silence … "see you soon." Click, phone down.

I found out sometime later that what I'd said shocked her, and it was completely unanticipated. This seems like an unnatural reaction to a deep emotion which had been sitting for so long and was straight from the heart.

15 | Meeting Up

I certainly wasn't weaponizing my statement. Once again, the gap in our lives played out as though we were strangers. This had a profound effect and became part of the learning experience of meeting the adult, as opposed to the child, you'd given up.

I knew exactly what it felt like to put the walls up for self-protection, but to have the walls put up to protect herself from *us* was something I had not expected. One would hope to build a relationship from the point of meeting forward, but unfortunately this isn't always the case. There was a relationship of sorts, but it might be nowhere close to what we hoped for.

I retreated upstairs and went to our bedroom, closed the door and broke down. I'd never been much one for tears as, having hardened up, that particular emotional reaction had left me long ago. But tonight was different; I cried tears for our meeting and I cried the tears of loss and anguish. I cried because I wasn't sure if I'd pushed the boundaries too far in telling her I loved her. I cried because I wasn't that sure we'd see each other again. It felt strange, but it was much needed, years of built-up tension needed to be released and the gates of the weir were fully open.

This was a day I was never going to forget either. It was wonderful and magical, best day of my life really. Who would have ever thought we'd meet the child who had been adopted—our hands forced by others—and who we thought we'd never ever see again. We thought for so long that it would never happen and yet today we looked each other in the eyes; you were mine and I was yours for a few fleeting moments. A father and daughter reunited. Wow.

16 | Meeting Up, Examined

What's it like meeting your daughter for the first time? I'm here, you're here, we've both turned up to look at one another and see what we find. It's a definitive moment in both of our separated lives. This time is ours alone. Your own flesh and blood. Someone you know to be yours, but not, at the same time. Someone you have wished to meet for all their life. It is a tricky scenario to play out and you are apprehensive, yet excited, at the possibilities. Open, yet guarded, as you are *so* conscious of saying all the right things.

My heart is exposed, I'm feeling vulnerable after being a closed book for all this time. There is no script for this. It's open and its raw. Is there a right or a wrong? It's confusing me already. Then there's the guilt and the shame that you hope she won't notice, or mention. It's like walking on eggshells while trying to maintain your balance. It's scary as hell because I have no idea, zero, of where it will go from here. Will it go forward at all? Will it be a disaster? Will she like me? I hope she likes me! What if she doesn't?

When we meet there is absolutely no denying that she is my daughter, she looks so much like me it is like looking in a mirror. Does she think the same and see our family resemblance? She is so enchanting, such a beautiful person in every way, so balanced, so sorted; and here I am trying to be 'as cool as a cucumber', but I'm completely and utterly overcome with emotion. I want to show some emotion, but then not too much as this might scare her away.

Do I laugh, do I cry, do I talk too much, or do I not talk enough? I don't want to appear aloof or up myself. What do I say, do I direct the conversation, or go along with the flow and see where it goes? Let her lead the conversation, don't press too many points, especially from the past. Questions, so many questions! How was her childhood? Was she happy in her family? What are her parents like? Are we like them? No, we couldn't be like them because we gave her away. More guilt.

Let her know I (we) never wanted to relinquish her. We were forced. Did she want to hear all of this? It is too early in the piece to be talking about this part. This is complicated. We hear her parents are lovely and I hear that voice in my head saying that we are not. Remnants from the past keep coming up in my thoughts, all the 'wrongs' are down to others because we are blameless, aren't we?

I know you, but I don't; I love you, but you don't know that. We are related but we're not, we're connected but we're not. There is a sense of a bond for me, how could there not be? But I'm not getting that back, there's distance, a short distance but a gap no less. How do we

16 | Meeting Up, Examined

mend that gap? I want to fix it right away and as soon as possible. Are we going to be close, is this the start of a friendship, a relationship? What is it we have? Nothing yet, we're starting from ground zero.

Time stood still, we talked and talked and then talked some more, who would know what about, I sure don't. There was no past, there may be no future, who knows, all we have is the NOW and I want to truly bask in these moments. I am emotionally and physically spent, drained of all energy, but I can't show her that either as that's negative, and this *has* to be a positive meeting, doesn't it? There's happiness and sadness, and wonderment, but there's grief too. There's joy and there's despair.

Comes time for you to leave. I don't want you to go, it seems we just got here, but go you must. We hug a long-lasting, meaningful hug and you drive away. Then the next surprise catches me unaware and the floodgates open. I cry rivers of tears and they just keep coming and I'm powerless to stop them. You are gone again.

17 | Where To From Here?

At the time of writing this in 2025 it has been thirty-five years since I met my daughter and a lot has happened. There's a lot of water gone under that bridge. There has been tension, friction, happy moments and sad moments, all part of life, I guess. I can say unequivocally it's definitely 'different' knowing an adopted child who is now an adult.

My three children grew up into beautiful adults, gained careers and left home. My father died in 2008 and that led me to make the decision to ask my wife, the mother of all my four children, for a divorce. I couldn't keep living the way I was as I was not at all happy. We'd both grown in different directions and wanted different things from life, so for both of us it was an amicable separation and we remain in touch.

Did having a child adopted at birth—forcibly removed—affect my life? That would be a definite yes. Does it colour my whole life experience? Yes, it does, and some of those experiences follow in this chapter.

Not long after meeting our daughter I gave her a gift of a clock for her twenty-second birthday. It was a beautiful timber Seiko desk piece, and it came with the message: *We have missed some of your life up till now so this clock is symbolic that from here on out all we have is time.*

I also started writing a book for her—a draft of this book, but thirty years ago. I felt compelled to write her the story of our lives from before she was born, what led to her being adopted and of those who influenced that decision. It was a review and an appraisal of where we had been and what was going on in our lives, to fill in the blanks for her.

The book was basically a timeline of our separated lives at certain ages or milestones, where we were in the world at those points in time, and what we had missed out on. She had also filled me in on important dates and times from when she was young, where she went to school, other important dates, and so on.

I told the truth, my truth at least, and passed the book on to my daughter. I'm not sure how it was taken as nothing has ever been said. It may have had a negative effect; it may have been triggering, but I will probably never know as there's been no feedback. My first draft is probably gathering dust in a closet somewhere.

In the early days of our new relationship, I had a sense of urgency to see her regularly on my own. I wanted her to know that she was always loved. I hoped I wasn't smothering her, but I had in my mind to make it very clear that she knew where I stood then, as now. I thought it was the very least I could do. I guess I was trying in my own way and in my love-language to reassure her. I was

17 | WHERE TO FROM HERE?

never sure how she felt about these interactions. I saw the people pleaser that I was in my early days coming through her now as she sat and took all this information in, but didn't say much. It was probably mind boggling for her, quite overwhelming.

The same application process to contact and meet an adopted child applied to Jan, one of Fran's older sisters. As mentioned in an earlier chapter, Jan had given birth to a son at Boothville Hospital many years earlier. Having seen how successful our reunion with our daughter was, Jan made a similar application and met her son some months later.

As I've said before, things don't always go the way one would hope for in these circumstances. Their relationship became fractious and we ended up having to cut ties with her son, as we thought his presence may have been damaging our relationship with our daughter. We were, if nothing else, very protective of our new relationship with her and no one was going to do harm to it on my watch.

Our daughter's older (and adopted) brother also applied for contact on the strength of our great reunion. Unfortunately for him it also did not go well. He met his birth mother who was happy to meet up for a one-time visit, but subsequently wanted little to do with him. Also, she did not want to reveal who his birth father was. Their relationship is still tenuous today.

Our daughter's adoptive parents provided us with

hundreds of photos, with the negatives so we could get photos printed of her childhood for ourselves. This was a most wonderful gesture on their part. It filled in some of the gaps and at least we could trace her childhood growing up in an island community. We printed out hundreds, put them in albums and sat looking through them intently.

We then met our daughter's adoptive parents and spent a weekend on the island and saw where she grew up in the idyllic surrounds of that community. What a stunning place to grow up. Sun, surf, beaches.

We all got on beautifully, a welcome addition to their family. It was all very nice, BUT we never talked to our daughters' adoptive parents privately or in any depth. There was always someone else around so the time never felt appropriate. We would have loved to have had a one-on-one conversation with them about why we gave her up. Who knows what they may have been told in the past by the Department of Childrens' Services? They may not have been told anything and may have just been happy to receive our child.

I'm not sure what our daughter had told them either after our reunion meeting. So, it all sort of hung in the air as the great unknown. It seemed that we would never get that opportunity. Our daughter's life and the wonderful person that she was, was certainly testimony to how she was raised, so maybe her parents felt no need to know.

It was evident how openly generous our daughter's

17 | Where To From Here?

parents were when they invited my parents to their place for a lunchtime barbecue some months after we had our reunion.

I was pretty apprehensive about the whole thing, but just decided to go with the flow on the day. I mean, you'd be a bit out of it if you thought there would not be high emotional stakes at work here.

Our daughter's father grew prize-winning orchids and gave us all a tour of his multiple nursery houses, which displayed hundreds of his lovely multicoloured plants. He showed us all a new cultivar he'd propagated to produce a new species, which he named after Fran. I can't overstate enough how caring this man was, what a sensitive and considerate gesture.

The day went well—it was all very nice, much of the talk centring around my daughter's wedding plans. For me, it caused a lot of anxiety just observing this most unusual interaction. It was the people who had forced Fran and I to give our child away meeting the kindly folk who had received our child as a thirteen-day-old baby and then raised her. It absolutely blew my mind, the past coming to meet the future and every point in between!

Needless to say when the day was over, this was one of only two points of contact the parents would ever have.

We tried to not be intrusive at the wedding and hung in the background at all times during the service and afterwards. I would admit it was the strangest sensation to be sitting in the aisles while she, looking stunning, was walked up the centre of the church with her father. Once again, I had to take what I got and bit my lip. This was indeed a highly emotional moment.

We were included in the group wedding photos alongside the adoptive parents, and we felt honoured and very proud, but it was also a tad strange to be in that position. We felt like we stuck out like sore thumbs, but we smiled for the cameras all the same because of the enormity of the occasion. We thought that all eyes would be on us with folk wondering who this other smartly dressed couple were! Some folk would have known, others wouldn't have.

Although not invited, my parents also attended the church for the ceremony only, and Dad commented to me on the uncanny resemblance our daughter had to our family. I would have loved to have known more of what they were thinking, as this was the second time— and the last time—my parents would meet our daughter's adoptive parents.

The reception was the usual for most weddings: drink, dancing, and food, but with the exception of one notable thing. During the speeches our daughter's adopted father thanked Fran and I, because without us she would not have existed. This was most humbling and heartfelt. It spoke of the enormity of the whole situation for us as her birth parents and for them as her adoptive parents. You could sense they felt they were losing her for the first time too, and they expressed this to us later

17 | Where To From Here?

as well.

A lot of her relatives introduced themselves to us during the night—it was lovely gesture that they were making themselves known to us.

A couple of years passed before our daughter announced her pregnancy to the world. A son, first born, followed in quick succession by a daughter and then twins over a five-year span. When the grandchildren were born, we were instantly termed as 'grandparents' by the other grandparents. Unfortunately, this did not sit well with us. We took it upon ourselves to tell our daughter that we'd prefer to set some ground rules and, in all cases, we wanted to just be known as Phil and Fran. I thought it was a stretch too far to be honoured with the title of grandparents and that the other grandparents were far more worthy of that than us. Part of our reasoning was to not confuse the grandkids themselves, even though they may have accepted it without a second thought.

This originates from the remorse we felt when our daughter was born and subsequently adopted. They might have seen this as folly or an oddity but it made perfect sense to us. This tradition has, for better or worse, continued with the birth of our five great-grandchildren, as we hold no 'grandparent' title for them either, a sad reality.

Backtrack to December 1995. We heard that Boothville, the Salvation Army Hospital, was to be sold. They would be holding two open days over a weekend for previous patients, mothers, etc., to view the inside of the house and walk the surrounding grounds and gardens. A week before the event Fran had phoned our daughter to ask if she would be interested in visiting the place where she was born. However, she was more than a little reluctant to commit herself, so we didn't push it and the day passed us by.

Come to think of it our daughter very rarely, if ever, committed to anything we suggested, so we backed right off and continued not to push the envelope. It would be a long five years henceforth before Fran and I would pluck up the courage to visit the house, and even then, just viewing it from the street was enough to tempt some forgotten feelings to the fore. The house is now privately owned, but continues to stand high on a hill in Windsor overlooking Brisbane as a monument to all who passed through its doors.

Almost three years later our daughter announced that she was again pregnant, and on the 30th of April 1997 a daughter was born. Our family visit to the Sunnybank Hospital the night after the birth had Fran and I feeling a little apprehensive as the newly arrived offspring was repeating history somewhat. A short time into our visit my newly-born grandchild was cradled in my arms, she was barely twenty-four hours old and she squirmed to find a position to make herself comfortable. I gazed into her little face trying hard to picture in my mind if this little child looked like the daughter I hadn't seen at this tender

17 | Where To From Here?

age. I was almost oblivious to whatever else was going on in the room and must have seemed pretty vacant as I sat trying to stir my thoughts.

Did she look like our baby at birth? I would probably never know, but this was the closest I was ever going to get to it and I didn't want to let that moment pass without etching it firmly upon my memory. The newborn was then passed on to her father as it was time for us to leave, visiting hours were well and truly over.

Our daughter's goodbye hugs and kisses are something we always look forward to, none more so than with this visit. When my turn came I told her, "I love you", as we embraced. We had often skirted around saying this outright to one another, and I feel the hesitance goes back to the day of our reunion seven years before with the phone call I felt compelled to make. We hug again as she replies to me in kind. I found myself reluctant to let her go and I wanted this closeness to go on forever. That is until I realise the bear hug I have clasped on her is beginning to startle her.

With my emotions well and truly risen to the surface, and my eyes filled with tears I face her to pronounce, "I've waited twenty-six years to see what you looked like as a baby ... and you were beautiful." We both knew exactly what this meant.

The twins were to come next in April 1999, a boy and a girl, a beautiful pigeon pair. That made four children under six years old.

18 | It's Not An Easy Road

A relationship with an adopted daughter can be complex, and to this day I do not understand where I stand in the scheme of things. It's quite disturbing and it NEVER leaves you alone, it's always there in the background. It's actually a sad way to live and it hangs over you like a cloud of despair. I should/could be bitter and twisted over what got us to this point but I'm not. Yes, I probably hold certain judgements against those who acted against me in the past because their actions defined me. They changed my life.

I often feel like I'm not my daughter's father, like I'm not a relative, like I'm not a friend, like I'm not family ... so where does that leave me? I'm a stranger to her. I don't really have a relationship with her children—my grandchildren—either. I'm just the dude who turns up occasionally to birthdays, funerals, etc.

She may see me as the guy who played a part and gave her away, and then to add insult to injury went overseas and had a great life on holiday all over Europe at her expense. Then we came home and started a whole new family, her real brothers and sisters, no less, without her. Even this is pure supposition, I don't actually know if that *is* how she sees things.

My daughter's husband has ALWAYS been there, there's never been a time when he wasn't there, so we've had zero quality time together. There are things I have never felt we could openly discuss with him around. He sees himself as her protector, her very own human shield even if she doesn't need one.

At family get togethers for the kiddly-winks' birthdays, and such, I often feel like a stranger who never quite fits in. There are always difficult introductions to other people. People always say, "Who are you then?" and I am left to explain myself. Even that can be confronting. I'll say I'm her *other* father and then you see their mind ticking over trying to work out what you just said. It's nearly always awkward. Sometimes they'll continue to talk to you and other times they are dismissive and just want to get away from you like you have the plague. It proves to be an interesting interplay. They either accept you or they don't, and you can read it a mile away.

I often leave these interactions feeling vacant, these are not the happy times that one would imagine. They are awkward times which pose more questions than answers and you still gain no quality time with your daughter. But you grab at whatever time you are given, the snippets of conversation in the 'busyness' of the event. You crave more, but get less because you withdraw, not wanting to rock the boat. You feel like you are forever on the outer and not within the inner circle of the family unit they have built. Oh yes, you don't fit, that's for certain.

18 | It's Not An Easy Road

I see that my grandchildren do not have a connection to my wider family, nor do they want to. There seems to be very little interest there from them. They are happy to have their family, and that's basically that. We don't have a deep relationship bond; it feels like there is an even bigger divide. I definitely see familial traits in my grandkids, but they seem oblivious to it. Maybe they will recognise these traits when they get older, and maybe then they will want to have more to do with us. Maybe it's too much for them to handle now. Maybe they don't require me or the complications I bring to their life.

The recent funeral of my daughter's adoptive father was particularly difficult for us, but my daughter wouldn't have known. We heard about his passing the day after he died, but in the days that followed, we were not officially invited to the funeral. We found out about the date and time through social media, not knowing if we should just turn up. As it turned out a small troop of Kenwards did attend and we were welcomed for our support. I was very conscious of that fact; we were just there to support our daughter.

Watching the slide show of her adopted family projected on the wall of the chapel during the service, seeing my daughter as a child—photos we had never seen—with another family, standing next to her dad. And there am I thinking she was so beautiful. Why couldn't I have brought her up? This hit me sideways and brought up so many unresolved emotions. I didn't cry, although tears could have been easily masked by the fact that we were at a solemn occasion. As always, I had to try and be strong under the weight of it all. It wasn't easy, in fact being at this funeral may have been one of the hardest things I've ever done. It was *so* challenging on many levels.

My mother being there did not make it any easier. On the surface it was a very nice gesture for her to attend ... BUT! There's a whole gamut of stuff going on here below the surface. *Wakey, wakey! My daughter, your actual grandchild, was adopted because of you, Mum, just in case you didn't realise. Her adoptive father, who adopted her because of your decisions, Mum, has just died. The grief I was feeling in that room was like a tidal wave about to wipe us out.* [Major anxiety at work here].

The problem is my mother had no idea about what was happening. She was blissfully unaware. She had no idea: not of the grief I have endured nor of the abandonment issues at play here. She lived—lives—in fantasy land that everything was as it should be and that my daughter had a wonderful life growing up on an island and was completely unaffected by her adoption.

This was complete bullshit and it just added to my increasing anxiety. I wanted to be respectful and stay in the background and make no fuss, then leave to let the family grieve. For my mother it's all, "Let's go for a nice cup of tea (at the wake) and everything will be fine."

She took nothing into account about how I might have been feeling, nor how my daughter might have been

18 | It's Not An Easy Road

dealing with her grief. I have fifty-five years of grief standing behind my shoulder, looming as a huge shadow, and she just wanted to play happy families. I would have preferred to have gone alone and not had my mother there. In fact, I thought it was pretty out of place for her to be there at all, but what do you say? You can't just attend these sorts of things unaware of what's gone before. Maybe this was the trigger for my daughter backing away more recently.

As a group we were not sure if we should attend the wake as it could have been family only, but we were invited in no less. The wake turned out to be another awkward interlude in the proceedings as many people asked who we were, so I had to explain once again. It seems to never end. What am I supposed to say? 'Her dad has just passed away and I'm her other dad, but I'm not, because our relationship is crap ...' It's all too clumsy and it's overwhelming me.

It must be said that it was obvious that my daughter worshipped the ground her adoptive father walked on ... and I agree with her completely. The same certainly would not be said about me. How does she view me? Probably as the dude who gave her up, of little consequence. Would she acknowledge me at my funeral? Would she grieve for me? I doubt that very much, but that's just me *projecting*.

Some weeks after the funeral, Father's Day came and went. She would normally send me a text or call me on the phone, wishing me the best, but it didn't happen this year. Was she too busy? Still grieving, no doubt; so, I felt once again that I had no right to be her dad. I wasn't important enough to rate a mention.

Or maybe it's a question of divided loyalties? From discussions with my psychologist, and from attending Jigsaw meetings and discussing this topic with adoptees, I have learned that many adoptees feel the pull between their adoptive parents and their biological parents. Even when the adoptive parents are both dead and gone. Could this be why my daughter is avoiding me, even if subconsciously, since her adopted father's death? Knowing this doesn't make it any easier though.

As mentioned before, I wrote her a timeline book. I did it so she would know her lineage and history—English stock—and what a huge family she had come from. I also created a family tree for her, but she took zero interest in it. She doesn't seem interested in knowing about her wider family.

We are currently living in a vortex. There's very little communication, no family get togethers. Our daughter and her family have closed ranks and are shutting us—me—out. I'm not sure if this is deliberate, or if it's the grief taking over. My girls also feel shut out. Presumably much of her feelings will be centred around abandonment, consciously or otherwise. Maybe she feels deserted, that she has been left here on earth by her adoptive parents to carry on alone. There is nothing

18 | It's Not An Easy Road

I can do to prop her up because I am not required. She will deal with her grief as best as she knows how.

Will the vortex continue? Will we ever get to have those father-daughter moments? There are still so many unanswered questions. Maybe, for our daughter, our relationship is just what it is, no more, no less. It may be all she wants and maybe she is happy with her lot in life. Who would know? Maybe she doesn't realise what she's missing out on.

Has her adoption impacted her own kids? More than likely, but how would I know? Is she at peace? I would only be guessing. Does she understand the narrative of our shared story? Does she understand her feelings? Has she ever had the courage to deal with them? Or do they just get locked away in a box that never gets opened?

Is she traumatised by her adoption? She must be, how could she not be ? If she is she's not admitting it. She probably wouldn't discuss it with me in any case. Yet another closed door.

19 | Where Do I Fit In?

Where do I fit in? I don't think I do! That's one hell of an opening statement and for me it's very real. The gap is widening instead of narrowing; we are further apart now than ever, and I don't know why. I don't control this; I have zero control over it.

I want to fit in, but then it's not actually determined by what I want, think, or feel. It's probably got nothing to do with me, nor is it my business. Sad but true.

The whole thing of meeting an adopted child as an adult is complex, it's fraught with unknowns, it's fragile, it's fractious, it's complicated. It leaves you with more questions than answers.

It's hard to convince myself that everything is okay. It doesn't feel okay. It actually doesn't sit right in my world. We should be close, shouldn't we? Am I the only adoptive parent who feels like this? It turns out I'm not—just ask the members at a Jigsaw meeting.

I also don't know what my daughter expected from our relationship. What *did* she expect? What does she want out of it? What does she think defines us as a father and daughter? Is she happy with where we are at? She is probably unaware of my feelings, and if she is aware, maybe she is pushing them away into the too-hard basket. I find all this very hard to deal with. It's just another cog in the wheel with which to beat yourself up. It's lasted all this time—thirty-five years—and it never leaves you alone. Always questions, and time is ticking on but we skirt around the edges.

Our relationship is not what I imagined it might be. The depth just isn't there, the deep-rooted connection she had to her adopted father was, and evidently still is, immeasurable. The love that she has for me is indeterminable. I cannot or should not compare myself to him, but that's easier said than done.

'The difference' is that on Father's Day my other kids will always go out of their way to see me, shower me with presents, dinner, and so on. They make me feel special; my adopted daughter doesn't. I consider myself lucky to hear from her at all on Father's Day. Her adoptive father was, still is, the one who is reserved for all of her special attention. I don't feel worthy, I feel like a second-rate citizen beside him, such is her obvious love for him. I don't hold this against either of them, though it's the price I pay.

Will she miss me when I'm gone too? She doesn't have much to do with me now, so why would she? I'm *just* her biological father and whatever difficulties that has presented her with.

It's a staged approach. So, you feel the loss of your child at birth, then for the next twenty-one years you grieve

19 | Where Do I Fit In?

that loss not knowing if you will ever meet again, but you never forget them. I loved her during all that time from birth to twenty-one, there is no doubting that. But she didn't love me because she didn't know me, I wasn't there, I wasn't even on the sidelines I was completely out of the picture. It was a twenty-one year gap and it's left a huge hole. That's not her fault though, and I'm not blaming her.

Then miraculously you meet her at a reunion when she is twenty-one. It's all very nice when you first meet but then almost straightaway you begin to feel the loss of the attachment you had hoped for. The gap is so huge its width is incalculable; it's an abyss that you can feel. It's a bit like an endless pool you are swimming around in and you can't reach the sides or the end, its palpable. Sometimes you are cruising doing freestyle and at other times you feel like you are drowning in that sea of emotion.

You move on hoping to get a handle on this and navigate your way around the awkwardness. But the distance, however big or small, is always there and there is no fixing it. It's an impossible fix.

So, you move tentatively forward, and time passes all too fast. Events such as Father's Day, Christmas, and Birthdays can be forgotten like you don't exist. I'm always confused how to react to this, and it becomes another stressor of the old feelings. It's like piling emotions on top of emotions that have never been resolved. It's far from normal but what do you do? You can't cry, 'What about me?', you have no right to feel that way.

It's also repetitious on a grand scale because it comes around every year. It comes as a surprise when I do hear from her and I think, 'Oh, she does care … a little.'

How does this all work? It's a minefield which never gets any easier to navigate. It works at the adopted person's discretion, then you comply by just going along and playing the game. Nothing too serious, nothing to rock the boat. You can't push either, that's the last thing to do: to be invasive.

We have had times along the way when we have fully acknowledged each other. In those moments it's like we definitely know who we are to one another. We are related, we are flesh and blood, we are connected. They have been fleeting moments where real love stands out as clear as a bell, and they are indeed incredible. Small moments where we have looked at one another in the eye and said, 'I love you', and known that it is fully accepted and completely true and honest. These moments are not the norm, they are far, far from normal. But they are moments of truth which are to be cherished. They are like a drop in the ocean and you clutch onto them and hold them in a grateful heart. The emotions are so strong you are almost fit to burst, they are joyful and so meaningful. The next one of these moments may not come for years and you wait, then

19 | Where Do I Fit In?

wait some more. These relationships are very good for building patience and resilience.

I know that my other adult kids love me and they know I love them; its unconditional. It's a very different love with my first daughter and me. It's like love on the surface with all sorts of connotations below, and an absolute plethora of unsaid feelings and mysteries which will probably never be unpacked.

I am beginning to understand that an adopted child may feel that my kids, her real brothers and sisters, were nurtured, whereas she might feel like she was discarded by us, even if that wasn't the case.

My other daughters are *innocents* in all of this and it has affected them immeasurably. They were always told as little ones that they had a big sister, but it's been the same for them, although they've known *about* their sister since they were little, they still don't know her as a *real sister*. She doesn't treat them as such, it's more like they are friends and not recognised as her siblings, in some sort of convoluted way. Both parties acknowledge one another as to who they are, but that's about it. There is distance between them as well. You can see she's close to her other sister though because they grew up together. I know my girls would love a close relationship with their older sister but it's unlikely to ever happen. It would seem that this is a regular theme for adoptees, it's all about self-preservation. I believe my daughter would be doing this subliminally and is probably completely unaware of the flow-on effect it is having. She has to protect herself at all costs.

My twin girls started travelling as soon as they could afford it and we encouraged them to go on adventures across the world and to expand their horizons. My son travelled to America on his own as soon as he turned eighteen. It has worked, and they do look at the world differently, as all travellers do. More expansively. There is a big wide world out there and it's not as bad as the media would have you believe. In my experience people from other lands are not dangerous.

Love to her may feel—and I'm only surmising here—like: 'My mother who loved me gave me away because, even though she wanted the best for me, she wasn't able to look after me.' But it also leaves her with a feeling of rejection; she was given up after all.

She may also be feeling deserted by the loss of her adoptive parents, both having recently passed. So, abandonment figures a lot in these situations.

She currently has no time for us, and this has always seemed to be the way. She has never been to the house that I've lived in for the last nine years even though she has been invited. I lived in my previous residence for nineteen years and I don't remember her ever visiting it either. If you make yourself busy, you don't have to deal with the stuff on the peripherals. This is her safety mechanism. The push-pull of a relationship which is uncharted.

19 | Where Do I Fit In?

You get a different perspective from an adoptee's point of view, they are all about keeping themselves safe! Above all else. *'Getting too involved with these people, actual birth parents and family, could be dangerous and bring unwanted emotions or fears. I may be rejected again, so I have to protect myself from this.'* It may be a real fear, or it could be coming from a subconscious fear and it's unintentional. So, it is what it is. You get what you're given, and you take what you gets, joyfully.

Her mother, Fran, has struggled with this too. I fully acknowledge that she was traumatised by the whole process, and it made her into the person she is, the same as for me. I have, however, been open enough to deal with what I went through by getting counselling with a psychologist.

For myself, maybe I just have to accept what our relationship is and that's ya lot. There is no more. Who knows, because I don't.

For my part it's all about unfulfilled expectations. I fully expected my daughter, my first born, and I to have a loving father and daughter relationship, much like the one I enjoy with my two other daughters. But that is not what we have at all. It's nothing like it and it is *so* disappointing from every perspective. And on top of that there is nothing I can do about it. Nothing, Zero, Nyet— not happening.

Should I lower my expectations, is that the way around it? Am I supposed to just get over it after all this time, thirty-five years, and say, "Hey Hoo, that's the way it is, that's fine; get on with your life and I'll get on with mine"? It's extremely hard to do that. I've tried it. And then we go around in circles again. The constant roundabout at the fair ground, round and round we go. And life passes even faster every year. How do you tell yourself, "Oh well, my daughter wants bugger all to do with me."? Impossible, methinks.

Someone from Jigsaw Qld said at an Adoptees Group meeting recently, "Don't disregard your daughter, you just have to hang in and be there." And she should know as she was adopted in 1971 herself, so she's been there and done that. She has the experience of real life. Right. So that in itself takes a shed load of patience and a very different mindset to put yourself into. You think, 'Well here I am hanging in there, but nothing ever comes of it.' You only get snippets. It's truly fucked up.

With my two other daughters we all know what we're going to get out of our relationship. There is actually *no* expectation at all, expectation doesn't even figure in it. I love them, and they know it. They love me, and I know it. It's all 'a given' and dare I say it is a 'normal' situation.

Those who have not been through this process will not have an understanding of this situation at all.

20 | Radio Silence

Maybe this chapter should come with a warning, it's pretty dark. Am I to be damned to a life of silence? The silence deafens me and makes my heart broody. The silence is thick and feels tangible. I feel like life is on hold, I cannot move forward nor back, I'm suspended in this fear. I get very emotional and want to cry often over what has—is—happening to me. This makes me feel weak and not in charge of my emotions because they just take over and I have very little control over what comes up. My mind is cloudy now the older I get, it's definitely not as clear as one would have hoped it would be. I find it hard to make decisions and I procrastinate a lot more than I'd like. It creates anxiety which periodically takes me over and I am unable to think clearly.

Dealing with the outside world is like this for me: I distance myself from people on purpose, there is a barrier there which no one can penetrate. I can definitely be indifferent. I'm open to a point, and then the book closes. No one passes the wall I have built for my protection; it's invisible but it's there, no less, surrounding me on all four sides, boxing me in tightly. The walls are crushingly close. No one can get in, but equally I can't get out—I'm trapped.

I need human interaction until I don't and it all becomes too much and I have to run, yet again, to find my peace and calm. Then I see their faults and everything is wrong in life. Everyone has problems, no one escapes. Its bullshit if they make out otherwise. The fuckers try me out and sometimes I unwittingly let them walk all over me. You just can't trust *hoomans*. My mantra has forever been, *You can't hurt me, I've been hurt so much more than this in my life, so go your hardest*. My faults are too many to mention and I wear them like a badge of honour. I'm the same as you but different too. The constant cycle, one day into the next, always wondering: have I done the right thing, am I doing the right thing? Life seems like Groundhog Day sometimes. Eat, sleep, rinse, repeat.

And to my eldest daughter ... dealing with the inside world, and my own reality: I've tried to get close but that's just not an option available to you. That's obviously the problem. I want to be close to you, but that's not something you can manage, so the barrier remains intact between us. Those impenetrable walls are there for your protection, to save you from something you imagine might create hurt or instability for you. It's okay, I actually do understand if that's what you need to do. I do it too, but for different reasons; I've been really, thoroughly hurt by people.

So, we both lead a lesser life—one more comfortable

20 | RADIO SILENCE

with what you can cope with. That's all it is, a coping mechanism to deal with the fear of abandonment for a second time. I would *never* abandon you, but you probably don't believe that because I abandoned you once before, didn't I!

When we do engage I could be judged if I do or say anything out of the ordinary, perhaps something you don't want to hear. You'd rather hear the nice things like how I've taken up dancing again, learning the steps, it's fun. Is that general enough? So many things will be left unsaid between us because that's the way it is. Niceties are all there is. Distance created and distance kept. The gap only widens.

I'll be gone before you know it; it's true you can't deny that, because time is racing away. The hands of time don't stop for the likes of us. The cycle of life—one leaves and another arrives—it's the way of the world. You wouldn't have had the chance to say what you feel because you are protecting yourself from me. And I haven't either because I'm so very scared to lose you again. So, what is there to say at the end? I love you. It's the simple truth. I've told you a hundred times before, but I don't know if it registers with you. My "*I love you's*" fall to the ground adding to those uttered before into a useless heap of nothingness.

The real love in your heart comes from those who brought you up, not by me who gifted you to them. I just sat at the sidelines waiting for your return, and I didn't know if you ever would. No one knows my pain, not one person on earth knows how I feel. They just cannot know its depth. Sometimes I consider I'd be better off 'as in not here'; they are fleeting thoughts, but they are there, nonetheless. They come to visit me and make me feel unwanted and unloved again, even though I know I am well and truly loved by those closest to me. Maybe that would fix it, and you wouldn't have to worry about me anymore or have to think about what 'nice' things we'll say next. Erasure wouldn't solve it though; I'll have to wait it out and endure more of the same until the real end comes.

Life is full of lessons, so am I supposed to have learnt one by now about you and me, the 'us' that exists on an existential plane? I hope it's not painful, my actual passing, I'd like to go nicely, quietly with no hoo-ha thanks. I'm not scared of it, it's part of the cycle of life, there is no escape. Maybe my passing would provide you some relief, you wouldn't need to deal with me anymore on any level. That sounds sad, but to me it's a reality. I'll be gone and inaccessible, and you can get on with loving the family you created.

21 | MENTAL INCIDENTALS

What follows is an account of what has shaped my life one way or another—from the past and into the present day.

It may seem a juxtaposition to the adoption story told here but, nevertheless, it forms part of my whole life story. After the adoption my life was hardly going to be a bed of roses, but we do the best we can in this thing we call life. Despite all our attempts to mostly live a happy existence there are experiences that come our way which trip us up.

The second time I thought about suicide was a few days after I broke up with a woman I had been in an on-and-off relationship for nine years. I say on-and-off because that's what it felt like. It was never really stable or solid; ninety-nine percent of the time I wouldn't have had a clue where we actually stood. I wanted a robust and consistent relationship—she did not!

She was a narcissist through-and-through, and she literally drove me to the edge through emotional abuse. That's what narcissists do, and it's *NEVER* their fault. See the upcoming section on The Narcissist.

I wasn't going to let her win though! I knew I was being played, it's also what they do and how they manipulate, it's part of their credo. They keep you hanging around while they stalk their next victim, then you get dumped.

I found her out; she was seeing someone else behind my back. She thought she could get away with it but I exposed her. We were living about an hour's drive away from one another, and caught up on weekends. This suited her to a tee.

I left her one Saturday night and rode my motorcycle back down the highway on a freezing cold night. It was about as cold as her icy response to the fact that she had another lover.

Within days an avalanche of texts and emails arrived in my inbox. Most were from her, deriding me and telling me how wrong I was and that EVERYTHING was MY fault. I also received one from her daughter, who I used to get on really well with, and one from a long-time nursing friend of hers. They didn't hold back to tell me what a bastard I had been to leave such a beautiful person. Wow, just wow! She'd obviously pulled the wool over their eyes as well.

For days I questioned myself if I had done the right thing. The answer to all those questions going through my mind always came back to a definitive *yes*. You cannot live with a narcissist. It's an impossible scenario, you have to leave them for your own sanity and well-being.

The only problem was that I let my ex-partner get into my head. She pervaded my thoughts and crept through the cracks and crevices. I don't know why this was and I

21 | MENTAL INCIDENTALS

couldn't even begin to explain the motives behind all of this, but once again I sank into a pit of despair. To end it all seemed like a viable option. I thought about how I'd do it, and I thought about all of my family I'd be leaving behind.

My psychologist received a text from me late on Christmas Eve 2018, it contained four letters: **H E L P.**

An hour-and-a-half's conversation on the phone soon afterwards and my feet were back on Mother Earth. We arranged a counselling session for a couple of days later after she reassured me that I could get through Christmas Day and be okay at the end of it. Confused still, I turned up to my psychologist's office on the wrong day. Her family were all ready to go out when I turned up a day early. She still saw me, and gave me an hour-and-a-half of her time for free, no charge. She set me straight that I had made the correct decision to leave. She added that I'd learnt enough lessons from this relationship, and now was my time to find myself. During visits to my psychologist over many years she'd often say I was there to press Ctrl-Alt-Del and reset my brain.

You see, when you have thought about suicide once it never leaves you alone from that point forward. There is often an awful noise that rattles around in your head and it pops up at the most inopportune times. The demon rests, but not for long.

The upshot of this episode is that I lost something, innocence, naivety, I don't know what it was but I've never been the same person since. When you go down into that pit you don't come back the same person, there is some collateral damage to your psyche. Something in the telemetry of your brain gets rewired.

I had a LOT of counselling over this stuff with my psychologist, many, many, sessions in fact over a period of years.

It's all The Rage

Then ... deep inside there is the rage. I know it's there, no one else does. No one else would even suspect it's there bubbling under the surface. It's unbounded anger.

One of my favourite songs is *Killing In The Name* by Rage Against The Machine. I feel this song, it resonates with me, especially when it says on repeat, 'Now you do what they told ya' and then at the end 'Fuck you, I won't do what you tell me'.

I don't feed the rage, it doesn't dictate to me, it's kept quiet and controlled. Anyone who knows me knows I have a big heart, one full of empathy; I am not a monster or a psychopath. I have good morals and values, and I am fully aware of how to set boundaries too.

I am also a yoga teacher and over a period of fifteen years of practice I know how to find calm. I have taught myself to be patient. I meditate on a daily basis which brings a level of calm, peace, and stillness with it every

21 | Mental Incidentals

day.

The rage I felt at age sixteen against the pastor of the church still resides within me. I can summon it if I want to, it's still there embedded in my being. If it comes up, it feels as real as the day it happened more than fifty years ago. Those same, very real feelings resonate through my body and my peace gets shattered, albeit momentarily, until I let it go again to reside in that rickety old filing cabinet from the past inside my head.

The Beast was also let off the chain in a moment of grief some years ago after my dad passed away. My sister, who is five years younger than me, and I have never gotten on, there has always been a level of aggravation between us since we were young. After Dad's passing, at a family gathering to arrange his funeral, I tried to extend an olive branch to her and I apologised for any previous misdemeanours on my part. It was a heartfelt and genuine peace-making gesture as far as I was concerned. She neither thanked me nor offered an apology in return. So, I waited and I waited ... but nothing came.

Eventually she proffered, "I have nothing to apologise to *you* for!" She looked at me with disdain, like I had just done something else wrong. I couldn't actually believe my ears. Nothing, not one word to appease the situation, no compassion. It was then that I hit the roof, the rev limiter hit the red zone. I exploded with a tirade, not of swearing or anything else but just in disbelief. I had never felt rage like this come to the fore previously and, thankfully, not since. It bubbled to the surface in that moment due to the circumstances of losing a loved one. It was easily quelled but, in essence, it's still there and the anger sits uncomfortably.

ANXIETY? WHO, MOI? ...NEVER!

You'd never know it because I mask it so well. I could, and do, stand up in front of a yoga class of sixty people on a weekly basis and not one of those people would know anything different. *Phil the Yogi, oh yeah, he's always calm and zenned out, apparently. You just have to look at his demeanor, the way he cruises into a room.*

My anxiety started in my teens, and was probably caused by other people initially, although it may have been ingrained already. Feelings of being alone, being shunned by an organisation such as The Boys' Brigade, having life dictated to me by others, not being able to make decisions for myself, being separated from my partner, losing control of everything that mattered to me. Becoming a father at sixteen years of age then losing that child, who I didn't even get to meet, to a broken adoption system. Anyone surprised I have anxiety?

What does my anxiety feel like? Like someone is pushing you from behind, you hurry up, your thoughts rush, but it's not someone pushing at all; it's coming from within. Jumbled thoughts where you just can't concentrate and it's hard to give attention to anything specific. Work

21 | Mental Incidentals

becomes more of a chore because you can't focus. Feeling like you have to sprint, a feeling of danger being imminent, of something chasing you. Feeling like you are *out* of control even if you are perfectly *in* control, it's a fine balance.

Breathless, breathing stifled, tight in the chest, it can exacerbate into bringing on an asthma attack. Heart rate can be elevated or conversely all over the shop. My heart rate ramps up and I can feel it belting hard in my chest, it's very difficult to slow it back down. Hot flushes. Shakes, nervousness, panic, dizziness. Feeling fearful—after all, anxiety is fear itself. Uneasiness, being unsure of what will happen, or when.

Anxiety can come at anytime, anywhere, without warning, but it can dissipate as fast as it came and quickly vanish. When that happens it leaves you with a feeling of, 'What just happened to me?'

What helps me? To acknowledge the feelings, to sit with them, and ask why I am feeling this right now. What can I do to make myself feel better about the story I'm telling myself right now? To realise that my thoughts are just thoughts, they are not real.

Tell myself everything will be alright, there is no present danger, I am not going to die, everything is fine. Calm, deep breaths, be mindful, be in the now, right in this moment: no past, no future, just the here and now.

Take my mind off my thoughts, do a physical activity, do something to take me away from those thoughts.

Engage in something completely opposite to where my thoughts were taking me. Talk to a trusted source or mentor, someone who is understanding and knows me, this will lighten my load.

The above examples demonstrate, to me at least, that I have suffered the long-term effects of PTSD from when I was sixteen years old. The trauma caused by all that happened back in 1970—relinquishing a child—still sits basically unresolved and still causes me grief some fifty-plus years later. I don't like the effects it's had, and I do all I can to not let these outcomes control me even though all three have shaped who I am.

People Pleasing (the subtle art of)

How do you know if you are, or are not, a 'people pleaser'? There are signs and signals along the way that will tell you.

Early on in my counselling sessions, my psychologist once asked me to divide a pie graph up into my allotted time over a twenty-four period. Work, family, chores, study, etc, etc. Think of that pie graph as portions of your time each day and separate sections of your life. Divide it up by percentage: I spend X hours at work, I spend X hours travelling to and from work, I spend X hours driving the kids to sports or dancing, I spend X hours cooking/cleaning/washing ...

You may be surprised just how much time goes into

21 | MENTAL INCIDENTALS

others and very little for your own well-being, we are all guilty of this especially where young children are concerned. Time just marches away on us and we become exhausted, but the work continues the next day and then the next. It's what we do, we carry on, forge ahead. It doesn't matter if you are male or female, we all have responsibilities.

Turns out that I was ninety-nine percent a people pleaser, unbeknown to myself. I was totally unaware of this and surprised that I had led my life up until this point of time for everyone else and made zero time for myself. This was about to change.

It took some mindfulness to break the cycle. It wasn't that I suddenly became selfish, it was more that I became aware. I found that to look after others appropriately, especially my own family, I needed to look after myself first. What's the point of trying to look after other's needs if you are burnt out and not coping? It just doesn't work, and the negative effect of tiredness and trudging ever onward is that it also breeds resentment because you have no time to meet your own needs.

Many of us are people pleasers by nature, it's probably a hand-me-down from our parents. As discussed earlier in the chapter 'The Resurrection', I wanted more than anything to please my dad, and I went out of my way to help him anyway I could.

As an adult I used to work as an Engineering Draftsman

in a drawing office. I'd work all the hours available to me and then some. It wasn't about making money for my own pleasure, it was about providing for my wife and three young children, and the new house we'd just had built. Yes, I had a mortgage like everyone around me, but I also had a wife who didn't work, so I was the sole bread-winner. So, what did I do? I worked even more hours; I sacrificed my time for her and the kids. I also sent them away on holidays to the beach while I stayed at work. I'd join them on weekends only, and I perceived I was doing the right thing.

When this wasn't enough, I ended up working two jobs: my usual daytime drawing work nine to ten hours a day, and then as a shelf filler at Woolworths supermarket a couple of nights a week. I was near to burnout and I was missing valuable time with my kids, but I thought this to be my duty. More people pleasing, you see.

There is also a nasty trap that a people pleaser can fall into when getting involved in a relationship with a narcissist. See the next section on this subject.

They will love you—in their own way—to death because you will do all it takes to please *them*. You become putty in their hands and so easy to manipulate. These relationships become fraught and you are better off not entering into one. Remember, it takes two minutes to get into a relationship and two years to get out of one!

Remember that narcissists are very tricky folk to be involved with and you probably won't realise for some

21 | MENTAL INCIDENTALS

time what they actually are, and how they are manipulating *you*! They direct your life, not the other way around.

What to do? Learn to say NO. Because people pleasers say yes to everything just to keep other people happy. My psychologist used to tell me that, *'No'* is a sentence. In other words, if you say no, there is no need to explain yourself any further or apologise for your decision. I used to randomly say no to my family at gatherings, and they'd say what did you just say that for? I'd say, "I'm just practising!" It turns out verbalising the word 'no' is empowering, it makes it easier to use when you feel you are doubting yourself but you really need to use it. Also, the more you use it, the more you are likely to use it.

Have an interest or a hobby to direct your time into? It doesn't have to be all-consuming but something that takes you away from the normal drudgery of work and life in general. Fitness and healthy activities would be my go-to, especially mindfulness and yoga. Outside activities, if possible, will always be better as nothing beats fresh air and connecting to nature, even in some small form.

THE NARCISSIST: IS NOT YOUR FRIEND

We've all met one in some shape or form. They dwell in the midst of us. Narcissists go after people pleasers because they are easy targets. And people pleasers are attracted to narcissists because they can be exciting people to be around. It's a bit like a moth being attracted to a flame, the only trouble here is that you *are* going to get burnt! They'll charm your socks off and stab you in the back all at the same time without you even realising it. They are not nice people and they are driven by their own self-importance. They are sinister, they go after what they want, they have no regard for any other person or their feelings. They will hurt you more than you will ever know, and they will leave you utterly confused and questioning yourself.

We all have narcissistic tendencies, every one of us, and most of us can control those traits, but some are much, much worse than others. Narcissists have a way of turning you inside out and upside down without you even realising what is going on. They are master manipulators, and you become their puppet. It's a slow cook process. They have zero boundaries; they treat others appallingly and expect you to back them in situations you wouldn't normally find yourself in or agreeing to.

They also use a process called 'gaslighting' in modern terminology. This is when they use a deceptive and systematic way to feed you false or misleading information. It's a form of control which ends with you questioning yourself and everything you know about them. It leads you to doubt yourself, your truth, your morals, and your standards because you are being presented with the exact opposite of that. Over time, the stories and perceptions shared by a narcissist can

21 | Mental Incidentals

become more complex, potentially causing you to question your own judgment while seeking clarity. It also erodes the trust you once had in yourself.

They have grandiose ideas about their position and status in life, they think they are better than everyone else. They think the world owes them. You can't live with them; there is no fixing them. You can't change them or influence them; they have their own trajectory. They'll treat you like a piece of shit one minute, and love you to death the next, in their own deceptive way.

Here's an example to explain what I mean. My narcissist partner of nine years and I went to her best friend's house for a party one night. Her friends were filthy rich: prestige cars, yachts, big house, and the rest. On leaving the party she said to me, "*This* is what I want!" In reply I said, "If this is what you want, then you are with the wrong guy."

She subsequently had an affair with her best friend's husband ... wonderful.

You cannot be in a normal, healthy relationship with a narcissist. A narcissist dictates the comings and goings in their relationships. The norm for them would be to use you up then get rid of you once you've reached your use-by date, while all the time being on the lookout for their next victim. This would normally be at a time when they have crushed you to a skerrick of your former self and then already be involved with their next target. Remember, they dictate the terms.

In summary, my experience with a narcissist shows several markers you need to know about.

Narcissists are dangerous for your well-being. They do not operate in a 'normal' sphere, their thinking patterns are far from normal. They start out in a relationship by building you up and praising you for even the most minor achievements, but once you are 'on the hook' their process to systematically tear you down begins. When they are done with you it makes you superfluous to their needs. Narcissists only ever take away; they do not give. They whittle away at your self-confidence and remove your sense of self-worth.

They will turn the tables on you. If you challenge them, they are always right and you are wrong, there is no winning in this situation. They do not back down either. They will try and separate you from your friends and family, quietly and covertly. They'll criticise your long-term friends, trying to get you to side with them. You will find that when a narcissist or toxic person no longer has control over you, they will try to control how others see you. It's a difficult period to get through because you presume *all* the friends you made as a couple might turn against you. Don't be surprised that some, but not all, will have also fallen under the spell of your 'narcy' friend and may react accordingly.

So, how do you survive a narcissist? This is where you have to trust yourself and go back to the basics of your morals and standards. Friends unfortunately do tend to

21 | Mental Incidentals

take sides, even if they say straight to your face that they aren't. Do not get involved in the tit-for-tat or rumours. Know what is coming, it could be a shit-storm of defamation where you are the culprit for all of the wrongdoings.

You have to trust in yourself and know that the lies and untruths being bandied about you are simply not true, they are a *fabrication*. You basically have to set your course, and stick to it knowing that your actions will out them. Remember, actions speak louder than words, your actions will show who you truly are, there is no need to prove yourself beyond this. Boundary setting also works really well in this scenario. Narcissists do not have boundaries, so make sure **you** do, and stick to them.

Narcissists are pathological liars in every sense of the word. They are basically out to destroy you while you are with them. They do not think on the same level as normal human beings, they think on a completely different level which is all about your coercion. When you leave them, they'll do all they can in their power to destroy you, especially amongst your friends and peers.

Remember, if you are easily offended, you'll also be easily manipulated by a narcissist. A narcissist will pick up on this very quickly. They will get to know you and all of your traits, both good and bad. They'll zero-in on your deficiencies and use them against you wherever possible. They keep tally and bring things up when you least expect it. They use the element of shock and surprise as well. And they'll do this all in the name of 'love' through their cunningness. They will have lulled you into a false sense of togetherness, and working as a partnership towards what you may have thought was a common aim. There is no 'common' aim, remember it's all about them, you are a pawn in their game of manipulation. There to be used and ultimately abused.

So, when recovering from an encounter with a narc, the biggest factor is to have a support mechanism. Be it family or friends you *will* need back up. Know who is in your corner and who has your back. Narcissists will try to get you to distance yourself from your people, thereby giving them more power. They work away at corroding your character, name calling, bringing you down. It's very subtle. Get help from sources you trust. Maybe engage a psychologist, as they have a deep understanding of these situations.

Narcs are very demanding of your time, space, and energy. The world revolves around them and them alone. Know these things and make sure there is always time and space for you to be true to yourself. Be on the lookout for narcissistic traits in people you engage with. They are very good at being the chameleon and changing colours to suit situations, be watchful, be on your guard. They are very good liars, so be mindful that they could be spinning you a line. Mystical thinking is their enabler. They will have you double thinking *all* the time, wondering what you've done, even if you've actually

21 | MENTAL INCIDENTALS

done nothing. Their thinking is fanciful at best. You will never have the upper hand. Know that if you do engage with a narc for any period of time that you will need recovery time to rebuild your life as their impact can be quite traumatic.

It could take years to get over a narcissistic relationship and to rebuild your self-esteem. Narcissists do not want to be in a relationship to serve *you*. They are only in relationships which serve their best interest. No matter how appealing a narcissistic person may be, it is better *not* to engage with such people. Your life will be much better without them in it.

In conclusion, the very real story here is I was caught up in a very toxic relationship, and I had known for an age that I had to get out. When I did leave she told me via email that I was a coward, pathetic and weak. This was just another typical narc put-down.

If you flip this scenario from my perspective, it took a great deal of courage to leave a woman I did actually love. It hurt to go, but I knew within my every fibre that I had to look after me.

22 | Feelings

Feelings ... *Nothing more than feelings* ... So how does it *feel* to be the relinquishing birth father of an adopted child? It doesn't feel good; I can say that right from the get-go. I have had a lifetime of experiencing guilt and shame, with a plethora of other emotions, most of which have not served me well. I met my adopted daughter when she was twenty-one years old, and those feelings didn't magically disappear at that reunion, or afterwards. In fact, I could categorically say they have exacerbated since then.

Uncertainty played its part, before, during, and after our meeting. It's still there today, ever present. I started this book using lyrics from the Pink Floyd song, *Comfortably Numb*, as a reference. I have, for all my life, felt comfortably numb.

I'd say I'm an odd bod. I'm not your 'standard' human male archetype. I'm usually placid and an empath, I'm also a male yoga teacher in a female dominated domain. Who would have thought, hey? Most people wouldn't realise that yoga was originally invented by men for men. It may be disconcerting for others close to me, but I'm actually perfectly fine on my own. I am happy, most of the time, and I have made myself this way because I can't see the point in being otherwise. I have been sad and experienced depression on some level, and I didn't like being in that black hole so I dug myself out of it. The method I ascribe to is: one step at a time, one day at a time. Get through one day, the next day's going to improve, and life does get better, but you have to realise it's a gradual process. I also subscribe to the theory of 'fake it till you make it', the results from this approach can be amazing.

I have a very slanted view on life as I know it. It's the only reality I know, it's how I was shaped, and it's how others treated me at age sixteen that has brought me to this point in my life.

I would hazard a guess that back in the '70s those people did what they did and had no idea of the consequences of their actions on my future. I have probably suffered PTSD, the side effects of which include massive periods of anxiety. Suicidal thoughts have followed me and never leave me to 'just be'. These thoughts are invasive and an affliction.

I'm okay with myself, I quite like that I am different and don't just go along with the crowd. In fact, I'm proud of that. I'm introverted at times and can be extroverted too; it depends on the situation and who I'm around. I don't trust many people either, so that colours my way of being. People have to prove themselves to me long before they gain my trust. I'm okay in a crowd or at gatherings, but I know when it's time to leave and look

22 | Feelings

after my own wellbeing.

I've had a *lot* of counselling, numerous sessions with my psychologist, over a period of probably ten years. I want to understand my feelings, I'm inquisitive by nature and I want to know why I feel the way I do and how I interact with others. Regardless of all those therapy sessions, we still didn't get to the root of the problem even though we dove pretty deep in.

My world changed when I rejoined Jigsaw Queensland in 2024 and started attending the local general open discussion groups in Brisbane on a regular basis. Finally, I met **my** people, finally others understood what I was feeling. The forum provides a platform for birth parents, adoptive parents, and adoptees to share their stories in a safe space. There is a genuine exchange of ideas, and inquisitiveness from all sides to hear other people's stories, including the tribulations the adoption process has caused.

I was welcomed into that group to provide my side of the story: the narrative of the surrendering birth father, is mostly unheard. It has provided me a substantial connection and has been one of the most important chapters of my life until now. I now understand the 'whys and wherefores' of the other side of the story from the adopted child's perspective. Up until this point I had basically no idea what my daughter would have been feeling, thinking, or otherwise. It was all a guess on my part and it would drive me to distraction. It also led me to imagine, presume, and project thoughts, fears and feelings, which was not good.

It has been an absolute revelation and it brought a modicum of peace to my somewhat chaotic thought processes. I am definitely more settled within myself about my relationship with my daughter, and I accept that this is how things are. I know now that I can't change or influence her in any way. I'm getting on with my life and she is getting on with hers. I have to be thankful for the minimal contact we do have. I'm pretty sure my daughter would actually be unaware of how I feel about all that has gone before in my life. She has never asked me how I feel about the past; it is possible she will never ask me about the effects the past has had on me. I guess she just sees me as I am, and accepts it. But as you know from reading this far, there is a much wider story to all of this. I am who I am, because of the past.

After reading the book, *The Primal Wound*, by Nancy Newton Verrier on understanding the adopted child, I now have an even better grasp of what's going on in my daughter's life. She may be completely unaware, and probably is from my observations, of what she's feeling, and acts as she feels directed by her consciousness. Her view of the world is obviously tainted by being an adoptee; whether she acknowledges that or not is entirely up to her. Her world must have been directed by feelings of abandonment and loss although, once again, I doubt if she acknowledges these feelings consciously or otherwise. My guess is that she pushes these huge

22 | Feelings

feelings down and suppresses them and just gets on with her life as it unfolds. She makes her life busy, this is not a criticism, just a fact.

There is also an interesting correlation here. After meeting many other birth parents, adoptive parents, and adoptees, I have learned that a common theme runs strongly through each of their lives. They *all* suffer from feelings of loss, fear, anxiety, rejection, and abandonment on some level. These strong emotions and intense feelings are brought to the fore by the whole process of the adoption.

For me personally, it is now accepted that birth fathers can also be caught in an unceasing state of unresolved anguish over the loss of their adopted child. The next biggest emotion to be raised here is REGRET. Every one of us involved in the adoption process feels a great deal of regret. I feel it every day that I was powerless to stop my daughter being adopted. I feel it also because our relationship is not what one would imagine it to be and is likely to not improve. Her birth mother, Fran, feels the same and wears this grief every day of her life too. My dad and my mother-in-law also said they regretted their original decisions to have our child given away, and then had to live with that.

The only trouble is that regret is a useless emotion, to hold onto. It gets you nowhere. I guess all one can do is to acknowledge the feeling and to recognise and accept it. Practicing self-compassion will help in all cases.

The biggest influence on our relationship, as a father and daughter, is the fact that we met when she was an adult. What went before that point has been lost into the most immense chasm imaginable. I didn't get to meet her as a newborn nor hold her in my arms; to cuddle and nurture her, I didn't get to know her as a child growing up. All of those defining moments are missing. Her life as a child was predisposed by growing up with adoptive parents who loved her in a beautiful island setting; a life completely different to what we could have offered her, had we been given the chance.

Our new life since we met has been a roller-coaster ride. It's been good, it's been bad, it's had it's high points and it's reached right down to the lows. There have been misunderstandings, and there has probably been intrusiveness on my part, but never intentionally. There have been beautiful moments and there has been great sadness felt between us. Don't get me wrong, it all started out positively from the day we met. In the following years, we had Christmases and birthdays together, celebrated children and grandchildren being born, but the wheel has turned and I feel the ill winds of change have descended upon us, and our relationship is floundering.

I have no explanation why this is happening, other than perhaps because of the loss of both of her adoptive parents in recent times, and it just leads to more heartbreak and confusion, for me at least. It could just be a fluctuation period we are going through or it could

22 | Feelings

continue this way. I'm mystified and will remain so until a positive change comes. Though it does seem to be the way my daughter wants it to be. The folks at Jigsaw know what this is like, I need to be patient, apparently, and not push the boundaries. It has been suggested that I might use this 'waiting time' to get **my** stuff in order. I know we've had good times before so maybe this is a little blip on the radar and a time for us to reset, and when she's ready we'll come back together stronger than before.

So, once again I wait ... I've been waiting all her life ...

At the moment I feel I am invisible in my firstborn daughter's eyes. It's a familiar feeling, because in the '70s I was also unseen by the pastor of the church, and by the congregation, and by the Department of Childrens' Services due process. I didn't have a voice or any say in proceedings back then either, so I have become used to the feeling of invisibility, of not being seen or heard.

When we do get together our meet ups are 'nice'. By that I mean surface level stuff. Nothing ever gets brought up, very little gets mentioned about sensitive issues: real world stuff. We're just nice to one another, nothing more, nothing less. We continue to walk on eggshells, dancing around one another. Then we go our separate ways and have very minimal contact afterwards, that's how it is. I can't push the envelope. I'm actually done pushing, it's not worth the mental anguish. It's acceptance of something, once again, out of my control.

Pseudo Dad-ship is like this. Sometimes, when I'm driving past your suburb en route to another destination, I'll think to myself I should just drop in and say hi. And then I remember your text message that said you are busy this weekend and you don't have time to catch up. So, I drive on, drive past.

And then I spend the next half-hour analysing my thoughts: Could I have just dropped in anyway? What sort of reception would I have received? Would you be pleased to see me or would you be put out that I called in unannounced? I know you are struggling at the moment too because you said you were in your text message. I would have loved to have called in, even just for five minutes and given you a big hug because I know you need it. I probably need it too if the truth is known—but then you might think that was weird.

You said you have family support, which is great. I take this to mean you have *your* family and that you don't need me. Which could be totally the wrong perception, but that's how it actually feels for me. So, we dance this dance some more and the game continues.

Grandchildren. At time of writing this, I have five grandchildren and five great-grandchildren. I don't have the relationship with her children and her grandchildren that I'd like to have. This is with the exception of my eldest grandson—he and I maintain regular contact and

22 | Feelings

share lots of things in common, including a love of all things mechanical. It must be in his genes and it's quite lovely. I remain hopeful and open to this happening with the rest of them too, someday.

I think I'm an interesting guy with a wealth of knowledge who is well travelled and could tell them a yarn or two if they had the penchant to listen. They may be following their mother's lead and may not want too much to do with 'that silly old bugger' me.

I've led a full life journeying all over the world to the United Kingdom, much of Europe, America, Mexico, India (by Royal Enfield) where I rode across the magnificent Himalayan mountains, and then later Thailand's Mae Hong Song loop twice by motorcycle. I've raced go-karts and motorcycles, built three sailing boats, won state titles on 16-foot Mosquito Catamarans which I also built from scratch. I've rebuilt and raced a vintage open-wheeler car at the Hillclimb. I've built an electric guitar from bare pieces of wood and then played it in the four-piece band I'm involved in. I'm a certified Personal Trainer and have been teaching yoga for fifteen years, so I know a thing or two. Who knows? I can't explain it; they are probably all too interested in what they are doing to take any notice of me. It would seem my life doesn't matter to them so they maintain a distance.

I do feel an urgency for some contact with my daughter, though, because I'm seventy-one now and time is ticking on, and I can feel my own mortality. I'd like to talk about these things before I die. I'm not one prone to nihilism and I'm not being morbid, but as every day is not a given it should be sooner rather than later. It's the very same fatalistic approach I had the day we met and I rang to say, 'I love you'. Things will be left unsaid and will be lost to the void; thirty-four years have passed already in what seems like a flash. The opportunity could be lost forever.

This book is a legacy, capturing what I might not get to reiterate otherwise. There are a lot of things I'd like to talk about openly and honestly. I'd love to say to my firstborn daughter: 'Are you okay? I mean, really okay with your life. Are you okay with the fact that I (we) were forced to give you up? How do you *really* feel about that? How has all of this affected your life?'

I don't want flowery answers though, I don't want an explanation just to please me or to make me feel better. I want real answers, in real time, in the here and now. So many questions, my friend. Probably none I'll ever get an answer to. I actually don't hold onto any hope of this ever happening, for me it's a pipe dream.

My mother—now there is a story all on it's own. My relationship with my mother who, is ninety-five years old at the time of writing this, has been fractious for as long as I remember. We get on okay, but that's where it stops; surface level niceties are as far as it goes and that's all I can manage. I find I can't be around her for too long at any given time either. She played a huge part in the decision to give our child up, along with the others involved. Does she regret this? Did she ever discuss this with my father back then?

I don't know, I'll probably never know because at her age I am not going to broach the subject and upset her. I'm sure she has no idea the effect giving up a child has had on my life and what I have had to endure. She would also be completely unaware of the trauma and deep issues my daughter would have from being separated at birth from her biological parents.

Not only did my mother assure me that, "You'll get over it," but another piece of wisdom she inflicted on me was, "You are too young to know what love is." Really? Isn't your first love the most intense love of your life? I wondered then, as I still do now, did *she* actually know what love was herself? It's pretty harsh to make your son give up a child.

My mother expected me (us) just to get on with our lives and forget it ever happened. Unfortunately for her, I do hold this against her and I have never forgiven her for it. She has never had any compunction to apologise to me or my daughter for this. My mother lives in a fantasy that everything is fine and dandy. It's not, but I'm not going to tell her at this stage.

Jigsaw Queensland is a post adoption resource centre, and they also do a series of podcasts for adoptees, birth parents, and adoptive parents. I decided late in 2024, after listening to another birth father's harrowing story, that I too had a story to tell. You can find that podcast under my name on the Jigsaw Queensland website or through Spotify. My daughter knows the podcast exists because I told her it had been released. Several of her family members have listened to it and encouraged her to do the same. At the time of writing, I don't know if my daughter has listened to that podcast.

In early 2025 I was approached by the CEO of Jigsaw Queensland to become a Peer Support Officer. I was one of a group of four people chosen for the role because I have 'real life' experience. I am very much looking forward to this role and hope I can be helpful to others navigating their way through the adoption journey, whatever angle they are coming at it from.

So, dear reader, there you have it. I have found writing this book cathartic, it has done me a world of good to get it all out in the open and release it.

The adoption process in 1970, and then the subsequent reunion with my daughter twenty-one years later, has had a significant effect on my life in every way. Early on, my mental health suffered significant damage. It definitely changed my perception of the world and the way I deal with every facet of life, especially interacting with others. It is still affecting me today some fifty-four years later, so it is ongoing.

Meeting my daughter, as an adult, provided challenges on a multitude of levels I never would have thought

22 | Feelings

possible in a father-daughter relationship. Despite all of this it has still been worth every single heartache, the anxiety suffered, and the trials that have been encountered, and I wouldn't change meeting her for the world. She is my flesh and blood, we are related, we are connected, I see myself in her. She is a wonderful, kind-hearted woman with a heart of gold and I'm so glad we know one another.

To my lovely daughter, Priscilla, I wish I had met you when you were born, things may have turned out differently if we had. I hope you get what you need from this book, and know that I have always truly loved you, no matter what.

23 | Epilogue

Imagine this scenario for a moment, if you will. It comes from an alternative universe, and another space and time continuum. Fran, who is pregnant at seventeen, has had nine months of being kicked to the kerb by everyone around her. She has until this point been publicly shamed by her family, friends, and the church and been shunned and hidden from view by society.

She is at Boothville Hospital, it is the 10th of November 1970, she has just given birth to an absolutely beautiful baby girl. The birth of this child was not easy, such an ordeal, such pain physically and mentally, and they all combine to take their toll. Afterwards, in quiet contemplation, she thinks to herself I am eighteen years old now, I can make my own decisions and I will not be coerced into giving up my baby no matter what pressure comes. She is going to go against all and sundry and make up her own mind.

She knows her partner, Phil, loves her, she's not sure about anyone other than him. Everyone else has been a bitter disappointment. He has been her biggest supporter through all that has been thrown up against them both. Everyone else seems to have discarded her along this journey. What if she decides to fight back and go against everyone and everything that has been driving her along this path? She contemplates the known facts that this child is a product of love, and they will continue to love her no matter what comes. No doubt times will be trying from here on.

Phil gets to visit Boothville and sees his baby some days later, he gets to hold her and to look into her adorable little face. Her eyes are brown, a definite Kenward trademark. There is connection here, the one that's been there ever since her conception and as she grew over the term of her gestation inside her mother. The feeling of delight as she moved her little body under his hand, a foot here, a hand there pushing and stretching on those special times they met in the city in secret. His heart is filled to overflowing with love never felt before. Such a strong union between a father and his offspring. Phil sighs with relief that his child will not be given away.

On viewing her newborn grand-daughter, Fran's mother, Emily, quickly concedes that she cannot give up such an adorable baby, her own flesh and blood. There is no argument here, this child is precious and must be looked after. Fran leaves Boothville with her baby girl eight days later. She has been staunch and has not signed any of the adoption paperwork put in front of her, even though there was a lot of pressure brought to bear by those in control.

Phil agrees with Fran's decision and backs her totally.

23 | Epilogue

Emily, Fran's mother, is a stay-at-home retiree with plenty of time on her hands, she is also well capable of looking after a baby girl, having raised five daughters of her own. Fran will return to work to support them as soon as practicable. Phil will be allowed to visit and resume their relationship and provide monetary support. He looks into his daughter's beautiful little eyes and only sees pure love reflected back. Fran's four sisters also kick-in by buying essentials and the load is spread between them all. They all want to babysit her, everyone adores Priscilla, she's such a happy and calm baby. Phil and Fran will be married within eighteen months, and they will live happily ever after.

On hearing the news, the pastor of the church is most put out. Phil's parents are too, but soon warm to the idea that it was a decision out of their hands, so they decide to support their eldest son, who they know is trying to do the right thing.

How much easier could this scenario have been? It doesn't take too much imagination to know it would have provided a far better outcome for everyone involved. It would have just taken some lateral thinking and hard yakka. We, as Priscilla's parents, would have put in the hard yards and done whatever it took to support our child. Everyone would have known this—it's what caring and compassionate humans do. We could have been a unit, a strong everlasting family, and proof that you can make anything come true if you want it badly enough. We would have grown strong together fired by the trials we had been put through and we three would have been inseparable and blissfully happy for the rest of our days.

Unfortunately, the story is a myth, a purely hypothetical situation, BUT anyone with half a mind could see there were definite possibilities ... if only ...

Afterword

I Am ... I Said

But I got an emptiness deep inside
And I've tried
But it won't let me go
And I'm not a man who likes to swear
But I never cared
For the sound of being alone

"I am" ... I said
To no one there
And no one heard at all
Not even the chair

"I am" ... I cried
"I am" ... said I
And I am lost and I can't
Even say why
Leavin' me lonely still

"I Am ... I Said" lyrics by Neil Diamond
Stones and *Hot August Night*
1971 © Universal Music Publishing Group

Resources

Jigsaw Queensland

For forty-nine years, Jigsaw has assisted all people affected by adoption, and the professionals who work with them. Jigsaw Queensland provides the following services via the phone, email, and if possible and appropriate, face-to-face (by appointment only):

Information, referral and support
- Search and reunion assistance
- Emotional support and assistance with record searches and family tracing
- Monthly Support Group meetings
- Newsletters

Contact Jigsaw on (07) 3358 6666 or Toll Free (Qld only) on 1800 21 03 13 or online www.jigsawqueensland.com

Forced Adoption Support Services

Jigsaw Queensland is funded by the Australian Government Department of Social Services to provide forced adoption support services in Queensland. Call 1800 21 03 13.

Other Contacts

If you need help or require assistance:

Lifeline call 13 11 14

Beyond Blue call 1300 22 46 36

About the Author
Philip J Kenward

Philip J. Kenward lives in Brisbane, Australia, and *Our Separated Lives* is his first book. It addresses the issue of forced adoption in Australia in the '70s, and gives a voice to all the fathers of those children.

At the time of writing, Phil has four children, five grandchildren and five great-grandchildren. He met his adopted daughter when she turned twenty-one after the adoption laws in Queensland, Australia, were changed to allow access between adopted children and their birth parents.

Phil was born in Hastings, England and emigrated to Australia in 1957 as a four year old, with his parents. Phil's career path has included being a Fitter and Turner, a Senior Mechanical Design Draftsman, and he is currently a Yoga Teacher. Phil originally took up yoga to de-stress from the pressure of work and he then became a yoga teacher to help others to find calm. He has been teaching yoga for twelve years and has a unique style in a female-dominated space.

Phil has always had a passion for music and plays the guitar. He built his own electric guitar from scratch and plays in a four-piece rock and roll band. Other achievements include rebuilding and racing a Formula Minor vintage open-wheeler racing car, and building and racing motorcycles and a Go-Kart (in Mt Isa). He also built a sixteen-foot Mosquito catamaran from timber and won a state championship race in it on handicap at Lake Cootharaba in Queensland.

Phil is well travelled and has spent time in New Zealand, England, Europe, and America. He is a lifelong, avid MotoGP follower; he rode a Royal Enfield motorcycle through India and up into the Himalayas; and he has toured Tasmania and Thailand by motorcycle as well.

Acknowledgements

From little things big things grow

From Little Things Big Things Grow
Songwriters: Kevin Carmody / Paul Maurice Kelly
1993 © Kobalt Music Publishing Ltd.

Me, write a book ... you are kiddin' me, aren't you? Who would have ever thought, hey?!

I would like to acknowledge all those people who have encouraged me and helped me to write this book to give fathers of adopted children a voice.

You all know who you are, and you should know that you played a huge part in bringing this book to fruition and helping me to realise a dream.

In particular I'd like to thank Cheryl, my best friend and confidante; this book would not be what it is without you (listening to me go on about it endlessly).

My two lovely daughters, Sarah and Anna, for their patience with me, and for their creativity with the front cover. You are the two most beautiful humans I know.

To my psychologist, I give thanks—you saved my life. You also taught me about how everything in life is a lesson.

Thanks, and much gratitude to Jo-Ann Sparrow, President, and Helen Angela Taylor, CEO, of Jigsaw

Queensland and to all the crew there for helping me to understand all that has gone before—and probably what is to come too. Finally, I saw the other side of the coin!

To the folk at the Department of Families, Seniors, Disability Services and Child Safety, who are helpful, understanding, and wonderful to deal with.

I'd also like to acknowledge the team at Disruptive Publishing, especially to my editor, Jo Scott, for all her hard work ('step away from the keyboard, Phil!') and to Deb Fay for bringing this all together.

Much love xx

What's next?

While this is Philip Kenward's first book it is unlikely to be his last. Phil already has plans for a second book, *Tall tales and true of a male yoga teacher,* which takes a sometimes light-hearted look at the challenges of being a male yoga teacher in a predominately female space. Expect to see more of Philip Kenward in print.

Namaste.

Get in Touch

Want to contact Phil or learn more about his yoga classes in Brisbane?

 www.mygloriousyoga.com

 https://www.facebook.com/MyGloriousYoga/

 yogiphil@hotmail.com

www.ingramcontent.com/pod-product-compliance
Lightning Source LLC
Chambersburg PA
CBHW051423290426
44109CB00016B/1411